NorthStar 1

READING & WRITING

THIRD EDITION

Authors	JOHN BEAUMONT
	A. JUDITH YANCEY
Series Editors	FRANCES BOYD
	CAROL NUMRICH

Dedication

We dedicate this edition to Debbie Sistino
for her tireless attention to all things
NorthStar. It wouldn't be *NorthStar*
without her. Thanks, Debbie!

–John Beaumont and
Judith Yancey

NorthStar: Reading & Writing Level 1, Third Edition

Copyright © 2015, 2009, 2004 by Pearson Education, Inc.
All rights reserved.

Pearson Education, 10 Bank Street, White Plains, NY 10606

Contributor credit: Cynthia Boardman

Staff credits: The people who made up the **NorthStar: Reading & Writing Level 1, Third Edition** team, representing editorial, production, design, and manufacturing, are Pietro Alongi, Kimberly Casey, Tracey Cataldo, Rosa Chapinal, Aerin Csigay, Mindy DePalma, Dave Dickey, Graham FIsher, Nancy Flaggman, Niki Lee, Françoise Leffler, Amy McCormick, Mary Perrotta Rich, Robert Ruvo, Christopher Siley, and Debbie Sistino

Text composition: ElectraGraphics, Inc.
Development Editing: Barefoot Editorial Services, Inc.

Library of Congress Cataloging-in-Publication Data
Northstar 1 : Reading and writing / Authors: John Beaumont, Judith Yancey.—Third Edition.
    pages cm
 ISBN-13: 978-0-13-338215-0
 ISBN-10: 0-13-338215-X
1. English language—Textbooks for foreign speakers. 2. Reading comprehension—Problems, exercises, etc.
3. Report writing—Problems, exercises, etc. I. Yancey, Judith. II. Title. III. Title: Northstar one. IV. Title:
Reading and writing.
 PE1128.B41 2015
 428.2′4—dc23

2013050583

Printed in the United States of America

ISBN 10: 0-13-338215-X
ISBN 13: 978-0-13-338215-0

3 4 5 6 7 8 9 10—V057—20 19 18 17 16 15

ISBN 10: 0-13-404974-8 (International Edition)
ISBN 13: 978-0-13-404974-8 (International Edition)

2 3 4 5 6 7 8 9 10—V057—20 19 18 17 16 15

CONTENTS

WELCOME TO
NORTHSTAR

A BLENDED-LEARNING COURSE FOR THE 21ST CENTURY

Building on the success of previous editions, *NorthStar* continues to engage and motivate students through new and updated contemporary, authentic topics in a seamless integration of print and online content. Students will achieve their academic as well as language and personal goals in order to meet the challenges of the 21st century.

New for the THIRD EDITION

★ Fully Blended MyEnglishLab

NorthStar aims to prepare students for academic success and digital literacy with its fully blended online lab. The innovative new MyEnglishLab: *NorthStar* gives learners immediate feedback—anytime, anywhere—as they complete auto-graded language activities online.

★ NEW and UPDATED THEMES

Current and thought-provoking topics presented in a variety of genres promote intellectual stimulation. The authentic content engages students, links them to language use outside of the classroom, and encourages personal expression and critical thinking.

★ EXPLICIT SKILL INSTRUCTION and PRACTICE

Language skills are highlighted in each unit, providing students with systematic and multiple exposures to language forms and structures in a variety of contexts. Concise presentations and targeted practice in print and online prepare students for academic success.

★ LEARNING OUTCOMES and ASSESSMENT

A variety of assessment tools, including online diagnostic, formative and summative assessments, and a flexible gradebook, aligned with clearly identified unit learning outcomes, allow teachers to individualize instruction and track student progress.

THE NORTHSTAR APPROACH TO CRITICAL THINKING

What is critical thinking?

Most textbooks include interesting questions for students to discuss and tasks for students to engage in to develop language skills. Often these questions and tasks are labeled critical thinking. Look at this question as an example:

When you buy fruits and vegetables, do you usually look for the cheapest price? Explain.

The question may inspire a lively discussion with students exploring a variety of viewpoints—but it doesn't necessarily develop critical thinking. Now look at another example:

When people in your neighborhood buy fruits and vegetables, what factors are the most important: the price, the freshness, locally grown, organic (without chemicals)? Make a prediction and explain. How can you find out if your prediction is correct? This question does develop critical thinking. It asks students to make predictions, formulate a hypothesis, and draw a conclusion—all higher-level critical thinking skills. Critical thinking, as philosophers and psychologists suggest, is a sharpening and a broadening of the mind. A critical thinker engages in true problem solving, connects information in novel ways, and challenges assumptions. A critical thinker is a skillful, responsible thinker who is open-minded and has the ability to evaluate information based on evidence. Ultimately, through this process of critical thinking, students are better able to decide what to think, what to say, or what to do.

How do we teach critical thinking?

It is not enough to teach "about" critical thinking. Teaching the theory of critical thinking will not produce critical thinkers. Additionally, it is not enough to simply expose students to good examples of critical thinking without explanation or explicit practice and hope our students will learn by imitation.

Students need to engage in specially designed exercises that aim to improve critical thinking skills. This approach practices skills both implicitly and explicitly and is embedded in thought-provoking content. Some strategies include:

- subject matter that is carefully selected and exploited so that students learn new concepts and encounter new perspectives.
- students identifying their own assumptions about the world and later challenging them.
- activities that are designed in a way that students answer questions and complete language-learning tasks that may not have black-and-white answers. (Finding THE answer is often less valuable than the process by which answers are derived.)
- activities that engage students in logical thinking, where they support their reasoning and resolve differences with their peers.

Infused throughout each unit of each book, *NorthStar* uses the principles and strategies outlined above, including:

- Make Inferences: inference comprehension questions in every unit
- Vocabulary and Comprehension: categorization activities
- Vocabulary and Synthesize: relationship analyses (analogies); comparisons (Venn diagrams)
- Synthesize: synthesis of information from two texts teaches a "multiplicity" approach rather than a "duality" approach to learning; ideas that seem to be in opposition on the surface may actually intersect and reinforce each other
- Focus on the Topic and Preview: identifying assumptions, recognizing attitudes and values, and then re-evaluating them
- Focus on Writing/Speaking: reasoning and argumentation
- Unit Project: judgment; choosing factual, unbiased information for research projects
- Focus on Writing/Speaking and Express Opinions: decision-making; proposing solutions

THE NORTHSTAR UNIT

1 FOCUS ON THE TOPIC

*CT Each unit begins with a photo that draws students into the topic. Focus questions motivate students and encourage them to make personal connections. Students make inferences about and predict the content of the unit.

UNIT **7**

WHAT NUMBER ARE You?

1 FOCUS ON THE TOPIC

1. How many brothers and sisters are there in this family?
2. Do you have any brothers or sisters? If so, how many?
3. What is a good number of siblings to have? 0? 1? More?

MyEnglishLab

CT A short self-assessment based on each unit's learning outcomes helps students check what they know and allows teachers to target instruction.

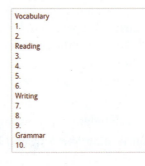

MyEnglishLab   Home | Help | Test student, reallylongname@emailaddress.com | Sign out

NorthStar 1 READING & WRITING

1   Unit 7

Check What You Know

Look at the list of skills. You may already know how to do some of these. Don't worry if you don't know how to do some or all of these skills. You will learn and practice them in Unit 7.
Check the skills that you already know. Put an *X* by the number.

Vocabulary
1. Use context clues to find meaning
2. Use idioms and expressions about families
Reading

3. Identify the main ideas in a reading
4. Scan a text to find specific information
5. Making inferences about how two people are similar or different
6. Understanding connections between nouns and pronouns, possessive adjectives, and *this/that/these/those*

Writing

7. Write a comparison paragraph
8. Organize ideas to make a comparison
9. Use words and phrases that show similarities and differences

Vocabulary
1.
2.
Reading
3.
4.
5.
6.
Writing
7.
8.
9.
Grammar
10.

*indicates Critical Thinking

2 FOCUS ON READING

Two contrasting, thought-provoking readings, from a variety of authentic genres, stimulate students intellectually.

TIMING IS EVERYTHING

1   Members of the same family have similarities. However, research shows that there are differences among oldest, **middle**, and youngest children. Scientists want to know: What are the differences and where do they come from?

The First Born

2   Oldest children are often very responsible[1] and organized. The reason is the parents. Parents **expect** the oldest child to be an example for the younger children to follow.

3   First-**born** children are often more educated than younger **siblings**. As a result, firstborns are more **likely** to have high-paying jobs. They become CEOs and doctors.

4   Firstborns get a lot of attention from their parents at an early age. However, they also have more **rules** to follow than younger children. For example, they have an early bedtime. New parents are usually **strict** with their first child.

---

[1] **responsible:** behaving in a sensible way and can be trusted

(continued on next p...)

CT Students predict content, verify their predictions, and follow up with a variety of tasks that ensure comprehension.

CASE STUDY: THE KOH FAMILY

1   Vincent and Helen Koh live in Arcadia, California. They have three children. They are all **adults** now.

2   Ellen, the oldest, lives in Arcadia. In fact, Ellen and her parents are next-door **neighbors**. Unfortunately, she does not see her parents often. She is the busy mother of three daughters. She is the CEO of the Arcadia Savings Bank. She also volunteers twice a week at the local hospital. These are only three of her responsibilities.

3   The Koh's middle child, Tim, lives in Los Angeles, about an hour away from his parents. He visits often and helps them with their computer problems. Tim is married to Sally. Their son, Steven, is in high school. Tim stays home and takes care of his family. He works part-time selling houses. Tim loves risky sports. He plays ice hockey once a week. Tim, his wife, and his son go skiing almost every weekend in the winter.

4   Jeff is the youngest. He is the "baby," but he is almost 40 years old. He lives in Philadelphia far away from his parents. Jeff got his Ph.D. in biology, and he is now a university professor. Like his sister, he also volunteers at a hospital. On weekends he performs[1] in a comedy club. He enjoys it. When he was young, he always made his family laugh. Now people pay him to be funny.

---

[1] **perform:** to do something to entertain people

GO TO MyEnglishLab FOR MORE SKILL PRACTICE.

CONNECT THE READINGS

STEP 1: Organize

Review the information of birth order in Reading One and the descriptions of the Koh children in Reading Two. Complete the chart. Then compare your answers with a partner.

IDEAS FROM READING ONE	IDEAS FROM READING TWO	
	TYPICAL	NOT TYPICAL
The First Born • responsible • organized • educated	Ellen is the oldest. She is very responsible and organized. She is a CEO of a bank. I think she went to college.	Ellen .....
The Middle Child • independent • looks outside the family for attention • "problem child" • problem solver		
The Baby • adventurous • artistic • funny • spoiled		

STEP 2: Synthesize

Work with a partner. One partner is Vincent Koh and the other is Helen Koh. Think about how your children fit (or do not fit) the ideas in Reading One. Use the chart in Step 1. Complete the sentences. Write about all three of your children. Then discuss your ideas with your partner.

_____ fits the description of a _____-born child. She/He
(name)   (first / middle / last)

_____ doesn't fit the description of a _____-born child.
(name)   (first / middle / last)
She/He _____

GO TO MyEnglishLab TO CHECK WHAT YOU LEARNED.

CT Students are challenged to take what they have learned and organize, integrate, and synthesize the information in a meaningful way.

MyEnglishLab

Auto-graded vocabulary practice activities reinforce meaning and pronunciation.

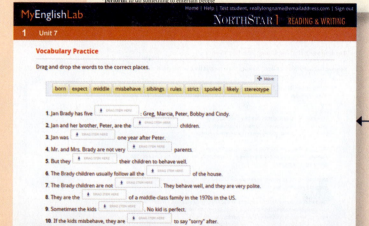

MyEnglishLab   Home | Help | Test student, reallylongname@emailaddress.com | Sign out

NORTHSTAR 1   READING & WRITING

1   Unit 7

Vocabulary Practice

Drag and drop the words to the correct places.

⊹ Move

born   expect   middle   misbehave   siblings   rules   strict   spoiled   likely   stereotype

1. Jan Brady has five [DRAG ITEM HERE] : Greg, Marcia, Peter, Bobby and Cindy.
2. Jan and her brother, Peter, are the [DRAG ITEM HERE] children.
3. Jan was [DRAG ITEM HERE] one year after Peter.
4. Mr. and Mrs. Brady are not very [DRAG ITEM HERE] parents.
5. But they [DRAG ITEM HERE] their children to behave well.
6. The Brady children usually follow all the [DRAG ITEM HERE] of the house.
7. The Brady children are not [DRAG ITEM HERE] . They behave well, and they are very polite.
8. They are the [DRAG ITEM HERE] of a middle-class family in the 1970s in the US.
9. Sometimes the kids [DRAG ITEM HERE] . No kid is perfect.
10. If the kids misbehave, they are [DRAG ITEM HERE] to say "sorry" after.

DETAILS

According to the reading, do these words and phrases describe the first-born (1), middle (2), or last-born (3) child in a family? Write the number on the line.

_____ adventurous   _____ funny   _____ left out

_____ oldest   _____ organized   _____ "problem child"

_____ problem solver   _____ responsible   _____ spoiled

_____ youngest   _____ more educated   _____ independent

CT Step-by-step instructions and practice guide students to exercise critical thinking and to dig deeper by asking questions that move beyond the literal meaning of the text.

MAKE INFERENCES

RECOGNIZING COMPARISONS

An **inference** is an "**educated**" **guess** about something. The information is **not stated directly** in the reading.

Writers often make **comparisons**—show how two things are the same or different. Sometimes these comparisons are not always directly stated. You have to make inferences to understand the comparisons.

A comparison sentence usually has two parts.

First-born children are often **more educated than** younger siblings. (paragraph 3)

A writer may not always include the second part (#2).

Look at the same comparison with only one part. As a reader, you have to infer the second part of the sentence to understand the comparison.

First-born children are often **more educated.** (**than** younger siblings)

Can you infer the second part of this example?

New parents are usually **strict** with their first child. (paragraph 4)

You can infer that the writer is comparing first-born children to later-born children. Here is the sentence with both parts:

New parents are usually **stricter** with their first-born child **than with their later-born children.**

READING SKILL

1 Look at Reading Two again. Then read the sentences. Choose the word or phrase from the box that means the same as the underlined word.

Ellen's	doing stand-up comedy	Tim and Sally's
Tim, Sally, and Steve	~~Vincent and Helen Koh~~	being a parent, a CEO, and a volunteer

1. They have three adult children. (paragraph 1)   _Vincent and Helen Koh_

2. Ellen and her parents are next-door neighbors. (paragraph 2) _____

3. These are only three of her responsibilities. (paragraph 2) _____

4. Their son, Steven, is in high school. (paragraph 3) _____

5. They all go skiing almost every weekend in the winter. (paragraph 3) _____

6. He enjoys it. (paragraph 4) _____

UNDERSTANDING WORD REFERENCE

A noun names a person, place, thing, or idea. A pronoun is a word that takes the place of a noun. When you read, it is important to connect pronouns to the correct noun. Understanding these connections can help you understand what you read.

Sometimes the pronoun refers to a noun in the same sentence. Other times the pronoun refers to a noun in an earlier sentence.

    Subject pronouns: *I, you, he, she, it, we, they*

    For example:
    They have three adult children. (*They* refers to *Vincent and Helen Koh.*)
    They all go skiing almost every weekend in the winter. (*They* refers to *Tim, Sally, and Steve.*)

    Object pronouns: *me, you, him, her, us, them*

    For example:
    He enjoys it. (*It* refers to *performing stand-up comedy.*)

There is also a connection between nouns and possessive adjectives (*my, your, his, her, its, our, their*)

    For example:
    Ellen and her parents are next-door neighbors. (*Her* refers to *Ellen.*)
    Their son, Steven, is in high school. (*Their* refers to *Tim and Sally.*)

The words *this, that, these,* and *those* make connections to ideas stated before.

    For example:
    These are only three of her responsibilities. (*These* refers to *being a parent, a...*)

Explicit skill presentation and practice lead to student mastery and success in an academic environment.

MyEnglishLab

Key reading skills are reinforced and practiced in new contexts. Meaningful and instant feedback provide students and teachers with essential information to monitor progress.

MyEnglishLab

Reading Skill: Understanding Word Reference

Read the text and click on the word, number, or phrase that the *pronoun* refers to.

1 On November 18, 1997, there were about 3,400 people in Carlisle, Iowa. The next day, *that number* (November 18th / 3,400) increased to 3,407. *It* (November 18th / November 19th) was a historic day.

Kenny and Bobbi McCaughey (ma·**koy**) had one daughter, Mikayla, but they wanted *her* (Bobbi / Mikayla) to have a brother or a sister. Unfortunately, it was difficult for Bobbi to get pregnant. Bobbi's doctor asked, "Do you want to try *fertility drugs?"

The doctor explained the risks of such drugs: The baby might not be healthy, or Bobbi might have a multiple birth. Kenny and Bobbi talked to each other. Then *they* (the doctor s / the McCaugheys) decided to take the risk.

After one month, when they visited the doctor again, *he* (Kenny / the doctor) told Bobbi, "You are going to have seven babies." Everyone was surprised and nervous.

The doctor explained, "*This* (visiting the doctor / having seven babies) is very dangerous," so Kenny and Bobbi talked again. Then *they* (the McCaugheys / the babies) said, "OK. They are all our children. *We* (Bobbi and Kenny / the children) want to try."

On November 19th, Bobbi had the babies—two months early. Forty doctors and nurses helped. In

3 FOCUS ON WRITING

Productive vocabulary targeted in the unit is reviewed, expanded upon, and used creatively in this section and in the final writing task. Grammar structures useful for the final writing task are presented and practiced. A concise grammar skills box serves as an excellent reference.

3 FOCUS ON WRITING

VOCABULARY

REVIEW

Complete the passage with the correct word from the box.

adults	confident	likely	misbehave	rules	stereotypes
born	expect	middle	neighbor	spoiled	strict

The Only-Child Syndrome

An only child is a person with no siblings. Some people think only children are selfish, lonely, or unhappy. They say it is difficult for an only child to play or work with others. This is called the "Only-Child Syndrome."

It is true that parents ___expect___ a lot from their only child—similar to the oldest child in other families. Only-children are often very responsible. They are also better at communicating because they speak mostly with ___2___ at home.

Like ___3___ children, only children are more ___4___ to make friends outside the home. This is natural. They need to play with other kids.

Like the youngest children, only children may be a little ___5___ by their parents. They get 100 percent of their parents' time and attention.

Some parents are ___6___—their children have to follow a lot of ___7___. But no child is good all the time. All children ___8___ sometimes.

(continued on next page)

What Number Are You? 157

GRAMMAR

1 Molly and Holly are sisters. Read the chart. Then answer the questions.

	MOLLY	HOLLY
YOUNG	is 25 years old	is 24 years old
TALL	is 5'2" tall (157 cm.)	is 5'7" tall (170 cm.)
FRIENDLY	is friendly	is a little shy
ATHLETIC	was in the Olympics once	watched the Olympics on TV once

1. Which sister is younger, Molly or Holly? ___Holly is younger than Molly (is).___

2. Which sister is taller? _____

3. Who is friendlier? _____

4. Which one is more athletic? _____

COMPARATIVE ADJECTIVES

1. Use the comparative form of adjectives to compare two people, places, or things. Use *than* when you are comparing two things in a sentence.	Holly is **taller than** her sister, Molly. Molly is **more athletic than** Holly.
2. For adjectives with one syllable, add -*er* + *than*. cool long old short shy strict tall young Notice the spelling change for adjectives that end in consonant-vowel-consonant: big → bigger thin → thinner	Molly is **shorter than** Holly. Holly is **younger than** Molly. Sydney is a big city. Tokyo is **bigger than** Sydney. Molly is **thinner than** Holly.

(continued on next page)

What Number Are You? 159

MyEnglishLab

Auto-graded vocabulary and grammar practice activities with feedback reinforce meaning, form, and function.

MyEnglishLab

Home | Help | Test student, reallylongname@emailaddress.com | Sign out
NORTHSTAR 1 READING & WRITING

1 Unit 7

Vocabulary Review 2

Complete the sentences with phrases from the box. Sometimes the form of the verb has to be changed.

| black sheep of the family   raise a family   sibling rivalry   take after   run in the ... |

1 Jan Brady thinks that she is the [____]. She feels different from her brothers and ... she isn't.

2 Mr. and Mrs. Brady wanted to [____] together.

3 The Brady kids play together a lot. Of course there is some [____]. But they do no... much.

4 Mrs. Brady has blond hair. The three girls also have blond hair. They [____] their ...

MyEnglishLab

Home | Help | Test student, reallylongname@emailaddress.com | Sign out
NORTHSTAR 1 READING & WRITING

1 Unit 7

Grammar 1: Comparative Adjectives

Drag and drop the words in the correct order to make complete sentences.

1 [is] [more] [staying at home.] [Traveling around the world] [exciting] [than]

[DRAG ITEM HERE]

2 [than] [adventurous] [his brother, Greg.] [Peter] [more] [is]

[DRAG ITEM HERE]

3 [athletic] [than] [more] [his brother, Peter.] [is] [much] [Greg]

[DRAG ITEM HERE]

Welcome to *NorthStar*   ix

A TASK-BASED APPROACH TO PROCESS WRITING

FINAL WRITING TASK

In this unit you read about stereotypes about birth order. You also read about the members of the Koh family.

Now you are going to *write a comparison paragraph about two family members.* They can be members of your family or another family. You will write about how they are similar or different. Use the vocabulary and grammar from the unit.*

PREPARE TO WRITE: Using a Venn diagram

A Venn diagram helps you to think about the similarities and differences between two things. In the center, you can list all the similarities. On the two sides, you can list the differences. The Venn diagram on page 163 describes Prince William and Prince Harry, pictured here.

* For Alternative Writing Topics, see page 169. These topics can be used in place of the writing topic for this unit or as homework. The alternative topics relate to the theme of the unit, but may not target the same grammar or rhetorical structures taught in the unit.

162   UNIT 7

CT A final writing task gives students an opportunity to integrate ideas, vocabulary, and grammar presented in the unit.

CT Students organize their ideas for writing using a particular structural or rhetorical pattern.

	Prince William Differences	Similarities	Prince Harry Differences

- was born in 1982
- is 2nd in line to be king
- married Kate Middleton
- has a son, Prince George
- many official responsibilities

- are the sons of Prince Charles and Princess Diana
- enjoy parties
- enjoy polo

- was born in 1984
- is 4th in line to be king
- is single
- has no children
- some official responsibilities

The Venn diagram makes it easy to see the similarities and differences between the two brothers.

1 Look at the information about Ellen and Tim. Then complete the Venn diagram.

Ellen
- Has a full-time job
- Thinks family is important
- Has three daughters
- Takes them to soccer and dance
- Spends time with them on weekends
- Eats out with them

Tim
- Has a part-time job
- Thinks family is important
- Has one son and wife
- Runs and skis with his family
- Spends time with his family on weekends
- Cooks and eats at home

Ellen Differences	Similarities	Tim Differences

What Number Are You?   163

Writing Skill: The Comparison Paragraph

Read the paragraph. Drag and drop the phrases into the correct categories.

Positive Sibling Rivalry

Venus and Serena William are famous tennis players. They are also sisters. They are from Palm Beach Gardens, Florida. Venus is older than Serena. Venus was born on June 17, 1980, and Serena was born on September 26, 1981. They both became professional players when they were 14 years old. Both are very talented. But many people think Serena is a better player than Venus. Venus was the #1 player in the world for a total of 11 weeks. Serena was the #1 player in the world for a total of 130 weeks. They also played against each other professionally 24 times. Venus won 10 times, and Serena won 14 times. There is some sibling rivalry between Venus and Serena. But they say that the rivalry is positive. The two sisters are good friends.

⊹ Move

played against her sister	was the #1 player for 11 weeks	was born on September 26, 1981
was born on June 17, 1980	was the #1 player for 130 weeks	thinks sibling rivalry is positive
won against her sister 14 times	became a professional tennis player at age 14
is from Palm Beach Gardens, Florida	won against her sister 10 times

---

MyEnglishLab

Key writing skills and strategies are reinforced and practiced in new contexts. Immediate feedback allows students and teachers to monitor progress and identify areas that need improvement.

---

2 Draw a Venn diagram in your notebook that shows the similarities and differences between the two people you are going to write about.

WRITE: Writing a Comparison Paragraph

A **comparison** paragraph shows the similarities and/or differences between two things. It uses examples to give the reader a clear picture of the similarities and/or differences. Like other paragraphs, a comparison paragraph begins with a topic sentence.

In a comparison paragraph, the topic sentence shows the purpose, or focus, of the comparison. It expresses the main idea of the paragraph. It tells the reader if the paragraph is about the similarities, differences, or both.

The body sentences give examples and details to show the similarities and/or differences. These details focus on specific **points of comparison** between the two things or people.

Example

> Ellen and Tim are siblings, but their weekly routines¹ are very different. Ellen has a full-time job. After work and on weekends, Ellen watches her daughters' soccer games or takes them to dance lessons. Ellen and her daughters often eat out during the week. On Saturday nights, they also like to make popcorn and watch movies. Unlike Ellen, Tim only works part-time, so he spends time with his son every afternoon. They like to run together. Every weekend they do things together. For example, they go skiing or play sports. Similar to Ellen, Tim has dinner with his family every night. He cooks, and they eat together at home. Ellen and Tim are very busy, but they spend their time in different ways.

The main idea of this paragraph is that Ellen and Tim do different things with their families. In this paragraph, the writer makes a **block comparison** between Ellen and Tim. First, he decides what he wants to compare—his **points of comparison**: their *work* and *activities*. Then he writes about each point of comparison—first about Ellen and then about Tim. The writer concludes the paragraph by returning to the main idea of the paragraph.

_____
¹ **routines:** regular way of doing things

A. Prince William

1. _____

2. _____

3. _____

B. Prince Harry

1. _____

2. _____

3. _____

3 Write the topic sentence of your paragraph about two family members. Be sure that it states the focus of your comparison.

4 Now write the first draft of your comparison paragraph. Start with your topic sentence. Then write sentences that give details and examples about the points you are comparing. Finish your paragraph with a concluding sentence.

REVISE: Connecting words to show similarity and difference

These words and phrases will help you connect ideas in your paragraph. Use a comma after each of these phrases.

SIMILARITY	DIFFERENCE
Similar to (name),	In contrast to (name),
Like (name),	Unlike (name),

Examples

Like Ellen, her parents live in Arcadia California. (They all live in the same city.)
Similar to Ellen, Tim has dinner with his family every night. (They both have dinner with their families but in different ways.)

Unlike most middle children, Tim enjoys playing risky sports.
In contrast to Ellen, who works in a bank, Tim works part-time selling houses.

Note that *like* means "almost exactly the same." *Similar to* is less specific. It does not mean "the same as."

---

4. (Like / be . . . years old) _____

5. (Your idea) _____

3 Now look at the first draft of your paragraph. Add connecting words to show similarity and differences.

GO TO MyEnglishLab FOR MORE SKILL PRACTICE.

EDIT: Writing the Final Draft

Go to MYENGLISHLAB and write the final draft of your paragraph. Check your grammar, spelling, capitalization, and punctuation. Check that you used some of the grammar and vocabulary from the unit. Use the checklist to help you write your final draft. Then give your paragraph to your teacher.

FINAL DRAFT CHECKLIST

❏ Did you write a comparison paragraph about two members of a family?
❏ Did you use a topic sentence?
❏ Did you use vocabulary from the unit?
❏ Did you have clear points of comparison?
❏ Did you use correct comparative forms?
❏ Did you use connecting words to show similarities and differences?

UNIT PROJECT

Work alone or with a partner. Research a famous family, such as a royal family, a famous family of actors, or a family on television. Follow these steps.

STEP 1: Brainstorm a list of famous families you know. Choose one to research.

STEP 2: Search online for information and pictures about this family. Read and take notes. Include important ideas such as names, ages, and important events in the family's life.

With instant access to a wide range of online content and diagnostic tools, teachers can customize learning environments to meet the needs of every student.

USING MyEnglishLab, NorthStar TEACHERS CAN:

Deliver rich online content to engage and motivate students, including:

- student audio to support listening and speaking skills.
- engaging, authentic video clips, including reports adapted from ABC, NBC, and CBS newscasts, tied to the unit themes.
- opportunities for written and recorded reactions to be submitted by students.

Use a powerful selection of diagnostic reports to:

- view student scores by unit, skill, and activity.
- monitor student progress on any activity or test as often as needed.
- analyze class data to determine steps for remediation and support.

Use Teacher Resource eText* to access:

- a digital copy of the student book for whole class instruction.
- downloadable achievement and placement tests.
- printable resources including lesson planners, videoscripts, and video activities.
- classroom audio.
- unit teaching notes and answer keys.

* Teacher Resource eText is accessible through MyEnglishLab: *NorthStar.*

COMPONENTS PRINT or eTEXT

STUDENT BOOK and

★ Student Book with MyEnglishLab

The two strands, Reading & Writing and Listening & Speaking, for each of the five levels, provide a fully blended approach with the seamless integration of print and online content. Students use MyEnglishLab to access additional practice online, view videos, listen to audio selections, and receive instant feedback on their work.

eTEXT and
MyEnglishLab

★ eText with MyEnglishLab

Offering maximum flexibility for different learning styles and needs, a digital version of the student book can be used on iPad® and Android® devices.

★ Instructor Access: Teacher Resource eText and MyEnglishLab (Reading & Writing 1–5)

Teacher Resource eText

Each level and strand of *NorthStar* has an accompanying Teacher Resource eText that includes: a digital student book, unit teaching notes, answer keys, downloadable achievement tests, classroom audio, lesson planners, video activities, videoscripts, and a downloadable placement test.

MyEnglishLab

Teachers assign MyEnglishLab activities to reinforce the skills students learn in class and monitor progress through an online gradebook. The automatically-graded exercises in MyEnglishLab *NorthStar* support and build on academic skills and vocabulary presented and practiced in the Student Book/eText. The teacher-graded activities include pronunciation, speaking, and writing, and are assigned by the instructor.

★ Classroom Audio CD

The Listening & Speaking audio contains the recordings and activities as well as audio for the achievement tests. The Reading & Writing strand contains the readings on audio.

SCOPE AND SEQUENCE

UNIT OUTCOMES	1 FRIENDSHIP WILL YOU FRIEND ME? pages 2–27 Reading 1: Welcome to the Friendship Page Reading 2: Facebook® Facts	2 ART ART FOR EVERYONE pages 28–53 Reading 1: Art for Everyone Reading 2: Looking at Haring's Art
READING	• Make and confirm predictions • Identify the main ideas in a reading • Scan a text to find specific information • Read large numbers and percentages MyEnglishLab Vocabulary and Reading Skill Practice	• Make and confirm predictions • Identify the main ideas in a reading • Scan a text to find specific information • Identify and use important numbers (ordinal numbers, cardinal numbers, and dates) MyEnglishLab Vocabulary and Reading Skill Practice
WRITING	• Write complete sentences • Put ideas in order **Task:** Write a paragraph about a person MyEnglishLab Writing Skill Practice and Writing Task	• Use time order • Use commas **Task:** Write a biography paragraph MyEnglishLab Writing Skill Practice and Writing Task
INFERENCE	• Infer information	• Infer opinions
VOCABULARY	• Use context clues to find meaning • Recognize and use word forms (nouns and verbs) MyEnglishLab Vocabulary Practice	• Use context clues to find meaning • Recognize and use word forms (nouns, adjectives, and verbs) MyEnglishLab Vocabulary Practice
GRAMMAR	• Recognize and ask and answer yes/no and wh-questions with the simple present of be and have MyEnglishLab Grammar Practice	• Write about events with the simple past of be and have MyEnglishLab Grammar Practice
VIDEO	MyEnglishLab Fans Forever–The Beatles, ABC News, Video Activity	MyEnglishLab Fish Artist, ABC News, Video Activity
ASSESSMENTS	MyEnglishLab Check What You Know, Checkpoints 1 and 2, Unit 1 Achievement Test	MyEnglishLab Check What You Know, Checkpoints 1 and 2, Unit 2 Achievement Test

3 SPECIAL POSSESSIONS
WHAT'S IT WORTH TO YOU?
pages 54–73

Reading 1: My Secret
Reading 2: Be a Smart Collector

4 BUSINESS
OPEN FOR BUSINESS
pages 74–99

Reading 1: Mom & Pop vs. Big Box
Reading 2: Etsy.com

- Make and confirm predictions
- Identify the main ideas in a reading
- Scan a text to find specific information
- Identify suggestions in a reading
MyEnglishLab Vocabulary and Reading Skill Practice

- Make and confirm predictions
- Identify the main ideas in a reading
- Scan a text to find specific information
- Use context clues to find the meaning of words
MyEnglishLab Vocabulary and Reading Skill Practice

- Write a topic sentence
- Stay focused on the main idea of a paragraph
Task: Write a paragraph about a special possession or collection
MyEnglishLab Writing Skill Practice and Writing Task

- Organize ideas to describe a place
- Use adjectives and prepositional phrases to describe a place
Task: Write a descriptive paragraph about a place
MyEnglishLab Writing Skill Practice and Writing Task

- Infer outcomes

- Infer tone

- Use context clues to find meaning
- Recognize and use word forms (nouns, adjectives, and verbs)
MyEnglishLab Vocabulary Practice

- Use context clues to find meaning
- Use gerunds as the subject or object of a sentence
MyEnglishLab Vocabulary Practice

- Recognize and use the simple present
MyEnglishLab Grammar Practice

- Recognize and use *there is/there are* and *there was/there were*
MyEnglishLab Grammar Practice

MyEnglishLab *Wedding Dress Crisis Averted*, ABC News, Video Activity

MyEnglishLab *Hawking Hot Dogs*, ABC News, Video Activity

MyEnglishLab Check What You Know, Checkpoints 1 and 2, Unit 3 Achievement Test

MyEnglishLab Check What You Know, Checkpoints 1 and 2, Unit 4 Achievement Test

---

SCOPE AND SEQUENCE

UNIT OUTCOMES	5 PHOBIAS **WHAT ARE YOU AFRAID OF?** pages 100–123 *Reading 1: Help! I'm Scared!* *Reading 2: Other Phobias*	6 ADVENTURE **WHAT AN ADVENTURE!** pages 124–145 *Reading 1: Lindbergh Did It!* *Reading 2: Crash Landing on the Hudson River*
READING	• Make and confirm predictions • Identify the main ideas in a reading • Scan a text to find specific information • Identify cause and effect MyEnglishLab Vocabulary and Reading Skill Practice	• Make and confirm predictions • Identify the main ideas in a reading • Scan a text to find specific information • Understand facts and opinions MyEnglishLab Vocabulary and Reading Skill Practice
WRITING	• Organize ideas to make a suggestion • Add supporting details **Task:** Write suggestions to someone who is afraid MyEnglishLab Writing Skill Practice and Writing Task	• Organize ideas in time order • Use time order words and expressions **Task:** Write a narrative paragraph about a trip or adventure MyEnglishLab Writing Skill Practice and Writing Task
INFERENCE	• Infer meaning	• Make inferences about people
VOCABULARY	• Use context clues to find meaning • Identify and use adjective + preposition phrases (e.g., *afraid of, embarrassed about*) MyEnglishLab Vocabulary Practice	• Use context clues to find meaning • Use synonyms MyEnglishLab Vocabulary Practice
GRAMMAR	• Recognize and use modals: *can, may, might,* and *will* • MyEnglishLab Grammar Practice	• Recognize and use the simple past (regular and irregular) MyEnglishLab Grammar Practice
VIDEO	MyEnglishLab *Unusual Phobias,* Healthguru, Video Activity	MyEnglishLab *Cockpit Cool,* ABC News, Video Activity
ASSESSMENTS	MyEnglishLab Check What You Know, Checkpoints 1 and 2, Unit 5 Achievement Test	MyEnglishLab Check What You Know, Checkpoints 1 and 2, Unit 6 Achievement Test

7 FAMILY
WHAT NUMBER ARE YOU?
pages 146–169

Reading 1: Timing Is Everything
Reading 2: Case Study: The Koh Family

8 SPORTS
HOW YOUNG IS TOO YOUNG?
pages 170–194

Reading 1: Ready Ronnie?
Reading 2: Evan Burch

- Make and confirm predictions
- Identify the main ideas in a reading
- Scan a text to find specific information
- Understanding connections between nouns and pronouns, possessive adjectives, and *this/that/these/those*

MyEnglishLab Vocabulary and Reading Skill Practice

- Make and confirm predictions
- Identify the main ideas in a reading
- Scan a text to find specific information
- Recognize the conclusion of a reading

MyEnglishLab Vocabulary and Reading Skill Practice

- Organize ideas to make a comparison
- Use a Venn diagram
- Use words and phrases that show similarities and differences

Task: Write a comparison paragraph about two family members

MyEnglishLab Writing Skill Practice and Writing Task

- Use expressions to give an opinion
- Write a concluding sentence

Task: Write an opinion paragraph about a young athlete

MyEnglishLab Writing Skill Practice and Writing Task

- Recognize comparisons
- Make inferences about how two people are similar or different

- Make inferences about people's priorities

- Use context clues to find meaning
- Use idioms and expressions about families

MyEnglishLab Vocabulary Practice

- Use context clues to find meaning
- Use idioms and expressions about sports

MyEnglishLab Vocabulary Practice

- Recognize and use comparative adjectives

MyEnglishLab Grammar Practice

- Recognize and use *very*, *too*, and *enough*

MyEnglishLab Grammar Practice

MyEnglishLab *You and Your Siblings*, ABC News, Video Activity

MyEnglishLab *Game On*, ABC News, Video Activity

MyEnglishLab Check What You Know, Checkpoints 1 and 2, Unit 7 Achievement Test

MyEnglishLab Check What You Know, Checkpoints 1 and 2, Unit 8 Achievement Test

---

ACKNOWLEDGMENTS

We would like to offer our sincere thanks to Carol Numrich and Nan Clarke for their insight and guidance.

—John Beaumont and Judith Yancey

REVIEWERS

Chris Antonellis, Boston University – CELOP; Gail August, Hostos; Aegina Barnes, York College; Kim Bayer, Hunter College; Mine Bellikli, Atilim University; Allison Blechman, Embassy CES; Paul Blomquist, Kaplan; Helena Botros, FLS; James Branchick, FLS; Chris Bruffee, Embassy CES; Nese Cakli, Duzce University; María Cordani Tourinho Dantas, Colégio Rainha De Paz; Jason Davis, ASC English; Lindsay Donigan, Fullerton College; Bina Dugan, BCCC; Sibel Ece Izmir, Atilim University; Érica Ferrer, Universidad del Norte; María Irma Gallegos Peláez, Universidad del Valle de México; Jeff Gano, ASA College; María Genovev a Chávez Bazán, Universidad del Valle de México; Juan Garcia, FLS; Heidi Gramlich, The New England School of English; Phillip Grayson, Kaplan; Rebecca Gross, The New England School of English; Rick Guadiana, FLS; Sebnem Guzel, Tobb University; Esra Hatipoglu, Ufuk University; Brian Henry, FLS; Josephine Horna, BCCC; Arthur Hui, Fullerton College; Zoe Isaacson, Hunter College; Kathy Johnson, Fullerton College; Marcelo Juica, Urban College of Boston; Tom Justice, North Shore Community College; Lisa Karakas, Berkeley College; Eva Kopernacki, Embassy CES; Drew Larimore, Kaplan; Heidi Lieb, BCCC; Patricia Martins, Ibeu; Cecilia Mora Espejo, Universidad del Valle de México; Kate Nyhan, The New England School of English; Julie Oni, FLS; Willard Osman, The New England School of English; Olga Pagieva, ASA College; Manish Patel, FLS; Paige Poole, Universidad del Norte; Claudia Rebello, Ibeu; Lourdes Rey, Universidad del Norte; Michelle Reynolds, FLS International Boston Commons; Mary Ritter, NYU; Minerva Santos, Hostos; Sezer Sarioz, Saint Benoit PLS; Ebru Sinar, Tobb University; Beth Soll, NYU (Columbia); Christopher Stobart, Universidad del Norte; Guliz Uludag, UFUK University; Debra Un, NYU; Hilal Unlusu, Saint Benoit PLS; María del Carmen Viruega Trejo, Universidad del Valle de México; Reda Vural, Atilim University; Douglas Waters, Universidad del Norte; Leyla Yucklik, Duzce University; Jorge Zepeda Porras, Universidad del Valle de México

WILL YOU
Friend Me?

1 FOCUS ON THE TOPIC

1. Look at the picture. What are the people doing? Check (✓) the answer(s).

    _____ studying   _____ looking at photos

    _____ talking to friends   _____ other: _____

2. What social media sites do you use? Check (✓) the answer(s).

    _____ Facebook®   _____ Twitter™

    _____ Pinterest™   _____ other: _____

GO TO MyEnglishLab TO CHECK WHAT YOU KNOW.

VOCABULARY

Read the sentences. Then circle the definition of the boldfaced word.

Bronwyn Polson started The Friendship Page, a website about friendship.

1. Bronwyn wants to help her **community** in Melbourne, Australia.

   A community is _____.
   a. all the people in one place
   b. all the people in the world

2. The movie last night was great! I **laughed** a lot. I was so happy.

   You laugh when something is _____.
   a. sad
   b. funny

3. On The Friendship Page, people write about their **goals**: a good job, a lot of money, a big family.

   A goal is _____.
   a. a problem you have now
   b. something you want in the future

4. When there is not war, people can live in **peace**.

   When there is peace, people are _____.
   a. happy and comfortable
   b. unhappy and angry

5. Karen likes The Friendship Page. She wants to **meet** new friends.

   When you meet people, you _____.
   a. call them on the telephone
   b. see or know them for the first time

6. If you have a problem, you can get **advice** on The Friendship Page. Then you feel better.

When you get advice, you get _____.

a. helpful ideas

b. money from your job

7. The Friendship Page is **safe** for young people. Bronwyn and her helpers watch The Friendship Page very carefully.

When something is safe, it is _____.

a. not dangerous to use

b. very easy to use

8. People on The Friendship Page like to **chat** about family, work, and friends.

When friends chat online, they _____ to each other.

a. write

b. visit

9. Your phone number is **personal**. You only give it to good friends and family. You don't give your phone number online.

When something is personal, you _____.

a. don't want everyone to know (about) it

b. tell a lot of people about it

GO TO MyEnglishLab *FOR MORE VOCABULARY PRACTICE.*

PREVIEW

Bronwyn Polson is from Melbourne, Australia. She started The Friendship Page (www.friendship.com.au), a website about friendship. Read this description of The Friendship Page:

> "Everything you want to know about friends and friendships."
> —The Australian Net Guide

Look at this part of Bronwyn's website.

Before you read, think about The Friendship Page. What is on this website? Check (✓) your ideas. Then read "Welcome to The Friendship Page."

_____ advice   _____ pictures

_____ chat   _____ poems

_____ email addresses   _____ songs

_____ information about Australia   _____ phone numbers

_____ people's real names   _____ other: _____

Now read part of the website.

The Friendship Page

1 Welcome to The Friendship Page—the website about friendship.

2 When Bronwyn Polson was 16 years old, she wanted to help her **community**. People **laughed** at her. They said, "You are so young!" But she didn't listen to them.

3 She was sure that friendship was important to everyone. So, in 1996, she started The Friendship Page.

4 The Friendship Page has two **goals**. One goal is to make the Internet friendlier.[1] The other goal is to bring more **peace** to the world. The Friendship Page is really about "peace through friendship."

5 Today, 25 volunteers[2] help Bronwyn with The Friendship Page. They all work hard, but they have a lot of fun. They think their work is very important.

6 The Friendship Page is very popular. More than 23,000 people in 200 countries visit every day. That's 8,000,000 people every year.

7 The Friendship Page is friendly, free, fun, and easy to use. You can make new friends. You can get **advice** about friendship. There are interesting pages with songs, poems, quotes,[3] and more. You can also **meet** new and old friends in the **chat** room.

8 People from 7 to 90 years old visit The Friendship Page. Most people are 13–34 years old. Young people and old people can be friends. They can help each other and learn a lot. Fifty-five percent are female, and 45 percent are male.

9 The Friendship Page is very **safe**. The volunteers watch the website carefully. They want it to be safe for everyone, especially for young people. They talk to the Australian police about Internet safety, too. On The Friendship Page, people do not use their real names. There are also no **personal** email addresses, no phone numbers, and no personal pictures. Also, when you delete information from The Friendship Page, no one can see it again. The information does not stay on the Internet. This is not true of some other websites.

10 If you are interested in friendship, please visit The Friendship Page at www.friendship.com.au.

---

[1] **friendlier:** more friendly
[2] **volunteers:** people who don't get money for working
[3] **quote:** someone's words

MAIN IDEAS

1 Look again at your predictions in the Preview section on page 6. Circle your predictions that match the information in the reading.

2 Read each sentence. Circle the <u>two</u> correct answers that complete each sentence.

1. According to the reading, the two goals of The Friendship Page are _____ and _____.
   a. to make the Internet friendlier
   b. to work very hard
   c. to bring more peace to the world
   d. to make a lot of money

2. The Friendship Page is _____ and _____.
   a. safe
   b. friendly
   c. difficult to use
   d. dangerous

DETAILS

Complete the sentences with the correct numbers from the reading.

1. The Friendship Page started in _____.

2. _____ volunteers help Bronwyn with The Friendship Page.

3. _____ people visit The Friendship Page every day.

4. _____ people visit The Friendship Page every year.

5. People from _____ countries use The Friendship Page.

6. People from _____ to _____ years old use The Friendship Page.

7. _____ percent are girls or women. _____ percent are boys or men.

MAKE INFERENCES

INFERRING INFORMATION

Some answers are easy to find because you can get the answer **directly** from the text. For example, is this statement true or false?

Bronwyn Polson's friends started The Friendship Page.

This statement is false. The answer is stated directly in the text. In paragraph 3 Bronwyn says, "So, in 1996, I started 'The Friendship Page.'"

Other answers are not easy to find because you cannot get the answer directly from the text. For example, is this statement true or false?

Some people don't believe that 16-year-old kids can help the community.

This statement is true. The answer is not directly in the text, but paragraph 2 reads: When [she] was 16 years old, [she] wanted to help her community. People laughed at her. They said, 'You are so young!'"

We read that people laughed. Also, we read that people said to Bronwyn, "You are so young!" We know that people sometimes laugh because they think an idea is funny or bad. Also, we know that some older people think that young people cannot do certain things. We understand—or **infer**—that some people <u>do not</u> <u>believe</u> 16-year-olds can help the community.

Read each sentence. Write **T** (true) or **F** (false). Look at the paragraphs in parentheses to help you find the answers. Then share your answers with a partner. Point to sentences that helped you find answers.

_____ **1.** Bronwyn believes that friendship helps the community. (paragraphs 2 and 3)

_____ **2.** Bronwyn believes the Internet is not friendly. (paragraph 4)

_____ **3.** Today, many people think The Friendship Page is a good idea. (paragraph 6)

_____ **4.** Some websites are not safe. (paragraph 9)

EXPRESS OPINIONS

Do you want to visit The Friendship Page? Check (✓) your answer. Then choose a reason or add your ideas. Share your answer with a partner.

_____ Yes, I want to visit The Friendship Page.

- I like to meet friends online.
- The Friendship Page is safe.
- I like the goals of The Friendship Page.
- Other: _____

_____ No, I don't want to visit The Friendship Page.

- I don't like to meet friends online.
- It is not safe to meet people online.
- I don't want more friends.
- Other: _____

Meeting a friend *online*

Meeting a friend *in person*

GO TO MyEnglishLab **TO GIVE YOUR OPINIION ABOUT ANOTHER QUESTION.**

READED

1 Look at the boldfaced words in the charts and think about the questions.

    1. Which of these words do you know?

    2. What do the words mean?

2 Read the charts.

FACEBOOK® USERS	NUMBER OF PEOPLE
number of **users** per month	1,000,000,000+
number of **users** per day	618,000,000+
0–24 years old	14%
25–34 years old	18%
35–44 years old	22%
45 years old or more	46%
males / men	43%
females / women	57%

PEOPLE USE FACEBOOK® TO . . .	NUMBER OF TIMES[1]
Listen to songs	22,000,000,000+
Find old or new friends	140,300,000,000+
Share personal photos	219,000,000,000+
"Like" a friend's photos or **updates**	1,130,000,000,000+

COMPREHENSION

Read the sentences. Write **T** (true) or **F** (false).

_____ **1.** 18% of Facebook® users are 45 years old or more.

_____ **2.** 43% of Facebook® users are males.

_____ **3.** People have shared 140,300,000,000 personal photos on Facebook®.

(continued on next page)

[1] total number since Facebook® started

_____ **4.** Finding friends is the most popular use of Facebook®.

_____ **5.** People have listened to songs more than 22,000,000,000 times on Facebook®.

GO TO MyEnglishLab *FOR VOCABULARY PRACTICE.*

READING SKILL

1 Look at the charts in Reading Two on page 11. Then check (✓) the true sentence.

_____ 618 million people use Facebook® every day.

_____ 618 billion people use Facebook® every day.

_____ 618 trillion people use Facebook® every day.

The answer is <u>618 million people use Facebook® every day</u>.

READING LARGE NUMBERS AND PERCENTAGES

When you read, it's important to understand numbers. There are different ways to write large numbers. They have the same meaning when you read them.

For example:
618,000,000 = 618 million
618,000,000,000 = 618 billion
618,000,000,000,000 = 618 trillion

You can also use a decimal point (.) to express large numbers.

For example:
140,300,000 = 140.3 million
140,300,000,000 = 140.3 billion
140,300,000,000,000 = 140.3 trillion

Percentages (%) are also numbers.

For example:
14% = 14 percent
22% = 22 percent

When we read percentages, we add the word *of*.

For example:
14% *of Facebook® users. . .*
22% *of people who use Facebook®. . .*

2 Look again at the charts on page 11. Use information from the charts to finish the sentences.

1. People have shared _____ 219 billion _____ photos on Facebook®.

2. _____ people use Facebook® every month.

3. People have "liked" a friend's photos or updates _____ times.

4. People have listened to songs _____ times.

5. _____ of users are 25–34 years old.

6. _____ of users are females / women.

■■■■■■■■■■■■■■■■■■■■■■■■■■■■■■■■■■■■■■ *GO TO* MyEnglishLab *FOR MORE SKILL PRACTICE.*

CONNECT THE READINGS

STEP 1: Organize

The chart compares The Friendship Page with Facebook®. Review Readings One and Two. Then check (✓) **Yes** or **No**.

	THE FRIENDSHIP PAGE		FACEBOOK®	
	YES	NO	YES	NO
HAS MILLIONS OF USERS PER DAY		✓	✓	
HAS USERS OF DIFFERENT AGES				
MOST USERS ARE 35 YEARS OLD AND LESS				
HAS MALE AND FEMALE USERS				
CAN FIND OLD AND NEW FRIENDS				
HAS SONGS				
HAS PERSONAL PHOTOS				

STEP 2: Synthesize

Use the information from the chart in Step 1 and your ideas to answer the questions. Write your answers on the lines. Then discuss your answers with a partner.

1. How are The Friendship Page and Facebook® the same?

   _____

   _____

2. Which website has more very young users? Why?

   _____

   _____

3. Which website do you like more? Why?

   _____

   _____

GO TO MyEnglishLab *TO CHECK WHAT YOU LEARNED.*

3 FOCUS ON WRITING

VOCABULARY

REVIEW

Read the paragraph on the next page. Then fill in the blanks with words from the box.

advice	~~goal~~	peace	users
chat	laughed	personal	
community	males	safe	
females	meet	updates	

At 16, Bronwyn Polson's _____ _goal_ _____ was to do something good for

her _____ 2. and for the world. Bronwyn called newspapers and social

service organizations, but they just _____ 3. . They said she was too

young to help.

So, she started a website called The Friendship Page. She believes in

"_____ 4. through friendship." Both _____ 5. and

_____ 6. use The Friendship Page. On The Friendship Page people

_____ 7. new friends. They can _____ 8. about important

things. They can share _____ 9. about new things in their lives. It also has

_____ 10. for people with friendship problems.

Volunteers help Bronwyn. They want The Friendship Page to be _____ 11.

for everyone. _____ 12. do not give telephone numbers or

_____ 13. information. The Friendship Page is a lot of work, but Bronwyn

enjoys it very much.

EXPAND

Study the chart. Pay attention to the boldfaced vocabulary from the unit.

Some words are *nouns*. A *noun* can name:	
a person	friends
a place	online, Australia
a thing	**update**
an idea	**peace, goal**
Some words are *verbs*. Most *verbs* show action.	**meet**
	chat
Sometimes a noun and a verb can have the same word form.	**update**
	chat
	friend
	laugh
Noun:	Bronwyn shares **updates** with her friends on The Friendship Page.
Verb:	Bronwyn **updates** her friends on The Friendship Page.

Read the sentences. Fill in the blanks with words from the box. Then check (✓) *noun* or *verb*.

chat	friend	laugh	update

1. a. Bronwyn and her friends are happy. They _____ a lot.

____ noun   ____ verb

b. Bronwyn has a nice _____. She sounds friendly.

____ noun   ____ verb

2. a. My family wants to know my news, so I send an _____ on Facebook® every day.

____ noun   ____ verb

b. My family wants to know my news, so I _____ them every day.

____ noun   ____ verb

3. a. I like Bronwyn. She is my best _____.

____ noun   ____ verb

b. I will _____ Bronwyn on Facebook®. I like her.

____ noun   ____ verb

4. a. My friend and I have a _____ every day on the phone.

____ noun   ____ verb

b. I _____ with my friend every day on The Friendship Page.

____ noun   ____ verb

Write three more sentences about people on The Friendship Page or Facebook®. Use one word from Review or Expand in each sentence.

Examples

People share personal photos on Facebook®.
My friend chats with me every night on The Friendship Page.

1. _____

2. _____

3. _____

GO TO MyEnglishLab **FOR MORE VOCABULARY PRACTICE.**

GRAMMAR

1 Read the questions (Q) and answers (A).

1. **Q:** <u>Is</u> The Friendship Page a website?

   A: Yes, it <u>is</u>. It <u>is</u> a website about friendship.

2. **Q:** Who is Bronwyn Polson?

   A: She is a young woman from Australia.

3. **Q:** Am I too young to help?

   A: No, you aren't.

4. **Q:** Does Bronwyn have a lot of friends?

   A: Yes, she does. She has a lot of friends on The Friendship Page.

5. **Q:** Do users have trouble using The Friendship Page?

   A: No, they don't. It's easy to use.

Look at the questions and answers in Exercise 1 again. Underline the verbs, including the helping verbs, twice. Underline the subjects once.

QUESTIONS WITH *BE*

1. For *yes / no* **questions**, use: the verb
be + **subject**

[verb] [subject]
Is The Friendship Page a website?

[subject] [verb]
Yes, it **is**.

You can answer *yes / no* questions with a short answer. Don't use contractions in short answers with *yes*.

[verb] [subject]
Am I too young to help?

[subject] [verb]
Yes, you **are**.
NOT: ~~Yes, you're.~~

[subject] [verb]
No, you**'re** not.

[subject] [verb]
No, you **aren't**.

2. For *wh-* **questions**, use: *Wh-* word + *be*
+ **subject**

[verb] [subject]
Who **is** Bronwyn Polson?

[verb] [subject]
What **is** The Friendship Page?

[verb] [subject]
When **is** your birthday?

[verb] [subject]
Where **are** they from?

[verb] [subject]
How old **is** The Friendship Page?

QUESTIONS WITH *HAVE*

1. For *yes / no* questions, use: *do / does* + subject + *have*	Helping verb [subject] main verb **Do** [I / you / we / they] **have** a lot of friends? **Does** [she / he] **have** a goal?

You can answer *yes / no* questions with a short answer.	**Does** she **have** a goal?
	    Yes, she **does**.
	    No, she **doesn't**.
	 Do you **have** a lot of friends?
	    Yes, I **do**.
	    No, I **don't**.

2. For *wh-* questions, use: *Wh-* word + *do / does* + subject	helping verb [subject] main verb What **does** The Friendship Page **have** on it? It **has** jokes, quotes, and much more.
Remember to end questions with a question mark (**?**).	helping verb main verb [subject] How many friends **does** she **have**? She **has** many friends.

2 Write questions about The Friendship Page. Then give your questions to a partner. Ask your partner to write the answers.

1. The Friendship Page / be / a website?

Is The Friendship Page a website?

2. Friendship Page users / have / personal webpages?

_____

3. The Friendship Page / have / a chat room?

_____

4. Bronwyn Polson / have / a goal? _____

5. What / be / Bronwyn's goal? _____

6. How old / be / The Friendship Page? _____

(continued on next page)

Will You Friend Me?   19

7. Who / be / Bronwyn Polson? _____

8. Bronwyn / be / from England? _____

9. Where / be / Bronwyn / from? _____

10. Bronwyn Polson / have / people
    to help her? _____

11. How old / be / you? _____

12. Where / be / you / from? _____

13. You / have / one best friend? _____

14. Who / be / your best friend(s)? _____

15. You / have / a personal webpage
    on Facebook®? _____

Your partner's answers:

1. Yes, it is. _____

2. _____

3. _____

4. _____

5. _____

6. _____

7. _____

8. _____

9. _____

10. _____

11. _____

12. _____

13. _____

14. _____

15. _____

■■■■■■■■■■■■■ **GO TO** MyEnglishLab **FOR MORE GRAMMAR PRACTICE AND TO CHECK WHAT YOU LEARNED.**

FINAL WRITING TASK

In this unit, you read about two websites where people meet and make friends.

Now you are going to *write a paragraph about a classmate and one of his or her friends.* Use the vocabulary and grammar from the unit.*

PREPARE TO WRITE: Interviewing

To learn about a classmate, you are going to do a prewriting activity called **interviewing**. In an interview, you ask questions. Then you use the information from the interview when you write.

Interview a classmate. Ask questions using the words below and the correct form of *be* or *have*. Write the answers in complete sentences on a separate piece of paper.

1. What / be / your name?

2. Where / be / you from?

3. When / be / your birthday?

4. You / have / a job? What / be / your job? Be / you / a student?

5. You / have / hobbies or interests? What / be / they?

6. Who / be / your best friend?

7. Where / be / he (or she) from?

8. How old / be / he (or she)?

9. Your friend / have / a job? What / be / his (or her) job? Be / he (or she) / a student?

10. What / be / his (or her) hobbies or interests?

---

* For Alternative Writing Topics, see page 27. These topics can be used in place of the writing topic for this unit or as homework. The alternative topics relate to the theme of the unit, but may not target the same grammar or rhetorical structures taught in the unit.

THE SENTENCE

1. A sentence is a group of words that expresses a complete idea. A **sentence** can make a statement or ask a question.

2. A **sentence** has a **subject** and a **verb**.	[subject] [verb] **Bronwyn is** a university student. [subject] [verb] **Volunteers help** with The Friendship Page. [subject][verb] **I want** to write a book about friendship.
BUT: In **commands**, don't use a subject (*you*).	[verb] **Send** me an email tomorrow.
3. The **first word** in a sentence begins with a **capital letter**.	**T**he website offers information and advice. **F**riendship is important to everyone.
4. Use a **period** at the end of a sentence. Use a **question mark** at the end of a question. Use an **exclamation point** at the end of a sentence with strong feeling. Do not leave a space before the **punctuation** at the end of a sentence.	The Friendship Page has fun information**.** Is this website safe**?** **Wow!** The Friendship Page is free**!** CORRECT: Do you use Facebook®? I love it. NOT CORRECT: Do you use Facebook® ? I love it .

1 Read the sentences. Underline the subjects once and the verbs twice. Add punctuation (a period, a question mark, or an exclamation point) at the end of each sentence.

> ### What Is Twitter _____
>
> Twitter is another popular website _____ Twitter started in 2006 _____ It is a lot of fun _____
>
> Users write messages to old friends and new ones _____ The messages on Twitter are called
>
> *tweets* _____ Are you interested _____ Visit Twitter online for more information _____

2 Look at each group of words. If it is a complete idea with correct punctuation and capitalization, check (✓) **sentence**. If not, check **not a sentence**, and change it to make it a sentence.

	sentence	not a sentence
1. My friend's name ^{is} Jane.	____	✓
2. Urville and Vera are from Chicago.	✓	____
3. Tony 23 years old.	____	____
4. Is a good student.	____	____
5. My sister likes Facebook®	____	____
6. He use Facebook®?	____	____
7. She has a lot of friends.	____	____
8. My brother my best friend.	____	____
9. We have fun on The Friendship Page.	____	____
10. we like reading the quotes.	____	____

3 Read the sentences. Find five more errors and correct them.

    ^M~~m~~y classmate's name is Bernard. He is 24 years old. He is from Senegal Likes

playing soccer and going dancing. Bernard's best friend Alexandre. he is from France.

He is intelligent and shy. He likes going to the beach and reading. Do you have any

questions to ask him.

4 Write the first draft of your paragraph about a classmate. Your first draft is the first time you write your ideas. Your first draft is different from your **final draft**. You will make some changes later. Use the information that you wrote from your interview on page 21. Begin like this:

> "My classmate's name is . . . He (or she) is . . ."
>
> OR
>
> "My classmate's name is . . . His (or her) friend is . . ."

_____

_____

_____

_____

_____

_____

_____

_____

_____

_____

REVISE: Ordering Your Ideas

A group of sentences about one main idea is a **paragraph**.

Read the paragraphs. Then answer the questions.

> The Friendship Page is very safe. The volunteers watch the website carefully. They want it to be safe for everyone, especially for young people. We talk to the Australian police about Internet safety, too.

How many sentences are in this paragraph? _____

People like to meet friends online. A lot of people like The Friendship Page and Facebook®. There are many other websites, too. People in China like Sina Weibo. People in Brazil like Orkut. People in Russia like VKontakte.

How many sentences are in this paragraph? _____

When you write your paragraph, you can organize the information in different ways. Here are two: (1) person by person or (2) by ideas.

1 Read Description One. It gives sentences about Fernando and then sentences about his friend, Ricardo. The order is "person by person."

Description One

My classmate's name is Fernando. He is from Spain. He is 21 years old. He is a student in Chicago. Fernando is friendly. He likes going to parties. Fernando's best friend is Ricardo. He is from Spain, too. He is 20 years old. He is a student in Madrid. Ricardo is friendly and athletic. He likes going to parties and playing sports.

2 Read Description Two. It gives information about Fernando and Ricardo together. The order is "by ideas."

Description Two

My classmate's name is Fernando. His best friend is Ricardo. Fernando is from Spain. He is 21 years old. Ricardo is also from Spain. He is 20 years old. Fernando is a student in Chicago. Ricardo is a student in Madrid. Fernando and Ricardo are both friendly. They like going to parties. Ricardo also likes playing sports.

3 Read both Description One and Description Two again. For both descriptions,

- <u>Underline</u> the sentences about Fernando.
- (Circle) the sentences about Ricardo.
- <u>Underline twice</u> the sentences about both Fernando and Ricardo.

4 Look at your sentences from your interview. Order your ideas. Number the sentences. Organize your sentences like Description One or Description Two.

GO TO MyEnglishLab *FOR MORE SKILL PRACTICE.*

EDIT: Writing the Final Draft

Go to MYENGLISHLAB and write the final draft of your paragraph. Check your grammar, spelling, capitalization, and punctuation. Check that you used some of the grammar and vocabulary from the unit. Use the checklist to help you write your final draft. Then give your paragraph to your teacher.

FINAL DRAFT CHECKLIST

❏ Did you describe a classmate and his (or her) friend?

❏ Did you use complete sentences?

❏ Did you order your sentences "person by person" or "by ideas"?

❏ Did you use *be* and *have*?

❏ Did you use vocabulary from the unit?

UNIT PROJECT

A **tribute** is something good that you say or write about a special person. Learn more about tributes and then write one. Follow these steps:

STEP 1: Go to The Friendship Page. Look at the Tributes Page— http://www.friendship.com.au/tributes/.

STEP 2: Read some of the tributes on the Tributes page.

STEP 3: Write a tribute about one of your friends or a family member.

STEP 4: Give your tribute to that person.

ALTERNATIVE WRITING TOPICS

Write about one of the topics. Use the vocabulary and grammar from the unit.

1. Bronwyn Polson has a goal. She wants "peace through friendship." She wants people to learn about friendship. What goals do you have? They can be big or small, for the world or for yourself. Write three to five sentences about one of your goals. Begin with: *"In the future I want to (be a doctor / write a book) . . ."*

2. Do you have friends or family who live far away? How do you communicate with them: by email or on the telephone? Write five sentences about communicating with these people.

3. Describe one of your good friends. Who is this person? Why are you friends? Look at the list. Check (✓) the most important qualities of your friend. Use your dictionary for help. Write five or more sentences about your friend.

Qualities of a Good Friend

_____ funny   _____ patient

_____ good-looking   _____ popular

_____ helpful   _____ talkative

_____ honest   _____ your idea(s):

_____ intelligent

_____

_____

_____

GO TO MyEnglishLab *TO WRITE ABOUT ONE OF THE ALTERNATIVE TOPICS, WATCH A VIDEO ABOUT FRIENDSHIP, AND TAKE THE UNIT 1 ACHIEVEMENT TEST.*

ART FOR Everyone

1 FOCUS ON THE TOPIC

1. What is the man doing?

2. What is his job?

3. Do you know this man? Who is he?

GO TO MyEnglishLab TO CHECK WHAT YOU KNOW.

VOCABULARY

1 Read the words and their definitions.

an ad

ad	short for *advertisement*; words or pictures that make you want to buy something
energetic	very active
famous	known by a lot of people
museum	a place to look at (not buy) art

drawing   a picture made with a pencil, pen, or chalk[1]

a drawing

painting   a picture made with paint

a painting

---

[1] **chalk:** Teachers use chalk to write on the blackboard.

sculpture   art made with wood, stone, or metal

a sculpture

public   for everyone to see or use

graffiti   pictures and writing made on public walls and buildings

graffiti

2   Complete each sentence with one of the words. You may need to use the plural form.

1. Keith Haring liked to work and play a lot. He was very _____*energetic*_____ .

2. The artists Picasso and Michelangelo are more _____ than Keith Haring.

3. Today, people can see Haring's art in _____ in Brazil, Europe, Japan, and the United States.

4. Haring also made _____ to sell things in magazines.

5. In the early 1980s, Haring made his art in a lot of _____ places in New York. He wanted everyone to see his art.

6. When he made a _____, Haring used different colored pens, pencils, and chalk.

7. Leonardo da Vinci's *Mona Lisa* is a _____.

8. Michelangelo's *David* is a very well-known _____.

9. Haring put _____ on the walls of buildings and in the subway in New York City.

▪▪▪▪▪▪▪▪▪▪▪▪▪▪▪▪▪▪▪▪▪▪▪▪▪▪▪▪▪▪▪▪▪▪ *GO TO* MyEnglishLab *FOR MORE VOCABULARY PRACTICE.*

PREVIEW

You are going to read a magazine interview. Before you read the interview, look at the timeline about Keith Haring's life. Then complete the chart.

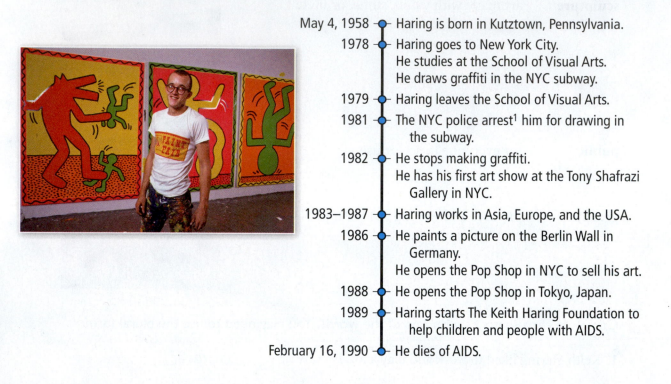

May 4, 1958	Haring is born in Kutztown, Pennsylvania.
1978	Haring goes to New York City. He studies at the School of Visual Arts. He draws graffiti in the NYC subway.
1979	Haring leaves the School of Visual Arts.
1981	The NYC police arrest[1] him for drawing in the subway.
1982	He stops making graffiti. He has his first art show at the Tony Shafrazi Gallery in NYC.
1983–1987	Haring works in Asia, Europe, and the USA.
1986	He paints a picture on the Berlin Wall in Germany. He opens the Pop Shop in NYC to sell his art.
1988	He opens the Pop Shop in Tokyo, Japan.
1989	Haring starts The Keith Haring Foundation to help children and people with AIDS.
February 16, 1990	He dies of AIDS.

What people, places, things, and ideas/activities were important to Keith Haring? Complete the chart.

PEOPLE	PLACES	THINGS	IDEAS / ACTIVITIES
			art

Now read the interview. Art World Magazine (AW) talked to Edwin T. Ramoran (ER) about Keith Haring. Mr. Ramoran is a DJ and an independent art curator in New York and Los Angeles.

---

[1] **arrest:** put in jail

ART FOR EVERYONE

Radiant Baby

1   **AW:** Mr. Ramoran, what kind of person was Keith Haring?

  ER: Haring liked people. He liked parties and dancing. He was **energetic**. You can see his energy in his art. His art moves and dances, too.

2   **AW:** When did Haring become **famous**?

  ER: In 1978, he started to make pictures in the New York City subway. Some people were very upset. They said, "This isn't art. It's **graffiti!**"

3   But graffiti *is* art. And some people like his art very much. They started to buy his **drawings, paintings,** and **sculptures**. Then galleries[1] became interested in his art, too. By the end of the mid-1980s, Keith Haring was famous around the world.

4   **AW:** What is Haring's art about? What does it mean?

  ER: When people asked Haring, "What is your art about?" he answered, "You decide." His art is funny, energetic, and sometimes angry. It is also political.[2]

5   His art is about education, freedom, and AIDS. These social issues were very important to Haring. His art is about children, too. He worked with kids on many projects. For example,

in the late 1980s, he made a large sculpture for a children's hospital in New York.

6   **AW:** Was Haring different from other artists?

  ER: Yes, he was.

7   **AW:** How was he different?

  ER: He was different in two ways. First, Haring liked to make art in **public** places, like in the subway. He believed "art is for everyone." In the early 1980s, he was famous for his public art. Later, he became famous in galleries and **museums**.

8   Second, he was different because magazines had **ads** with his drawings and paintings in them. People also bought his art at the two Pop Shops. At the Pop Shop there were T-shirts, watches, and buttons with his art. Nothing was very expensive.

9   **AW:** Is his art still popular?

  ER: Yes, it is. Haring died on February 16, 1990, but people still feel his energy in his art. Today we can see his art all around the world. Some of the money from his art helps AIDS organizations and children's organizations. His art still helps people. And if people want to learn more, they can go to www.haring.com.

10   **AW:** Interesting. Thank you very much, Mr. Ramoran.

  ER: It was my pleasure.

Untitled, 1984

---

[1] **gallery:** a place to look at and buy art. A gallery is also a room inside a museum.

[2] **political:** relating to politics or government of a country

MAIN IDEAS

1 Look again at your predictions in the Preview section on page 32. Add information from the reading to the chart on page 32.

2 Read each sentence. Circle the correct answer to complete the sentence.

1. In the early 1980s, Haring's art was in the _____ of New York City.

   a. hospitals

   b. museums

   c. subways

2. Haring's art was about _____.

   a. social issues

   b. his family

   c. famous people

DETAILS

Complete the sentences with the words from the box. Use each word only once.

ads	energy	money	social issues
decide	graffiti	public	

1. You can see his _____ in his art.

2. Some people said his work was just _____ and not really art.

3. First, he was famous for his _____ art.

4. He made _____ for magazines.

5. People asked, "What is your art about?" Haring answered, "You _____."

6. _____, like AIDS and freedom, were important to Haring.

7. Some of the _____ from the Pop Shop helped AIDS organizations and children's organizations.

MAKE INFERENCES

INFERRING OPINIONS

An **inference** is **an "educated" guess** about something. The information is **not stated directly** in the reading. Good readers put ideas together to find the right answer. Direct questions about main ideas and details are often easy to answer. **Inference** is more difficult. Writers sometimes do not state an **opinion** directly. You need to use what you know and information in the text to **infer** a writer's **opinion**.

Look at the example. Answer the question and read the explanation:

Do you think making money was important to Haring? Check (✓) your answer.

_____ Yes _____ No

In paragraph 2, we learn that he made art in the subway but not for money.
In paragraph 8, we learn that he sold his art at the Pop Shop but for low prices.

After reading closely, we **infer** that making money was not very important to Haring.

1 According to the interview, why did Keith Haring make art? Check (✓) the best answer. Look at the paragraphs in parentheses.

Keith Haring used his art to _____. (paragraphs 4, 5, 6, and 7)

_____ help his family

_____ communicate with people

_____ make a lot of money for himself

_____ pay for his art school education

2 Discuss your answers with a partner. Point out the sentences in the paragraphs that helped you find the answer.

EXPRESS OPINIONS

Give your opinion. Complete one sentence or both. Add your own ideas. Then share your opinion with the class.

I like Keith Haring's art because it is _____.

I don't like Keith Haring's art because it is _____.

GO TO MyEnglishLab *TO GIVE YOUR OPINION ABOUT ANOTHER QUESTION.*

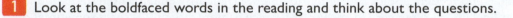

READ

1 Look at the boldfaced words in the reading and think about the questions.

1. Which of these words do you know?

2. What do the words mean?

2 Read the text and look at the art. As you read, notice the boldfaced vocabulary. Try to guess the meaning of each word.

LOOKING AT HARING'S ART

Some of Keith Haring's art was just for fun. Other pieces were about social or political issues. Here are two examples. First, in 1985, Haring made 20,000 *Free South Africa* **posters**—pictures or drawings made on strong paper and put on city walls. He wanted people to work together for freedom in that country. Second, Haring made *Stop AIDS*. That was in 1989.

The snake is a **symbol**, or image, of AIDS. The scissors are people working together to stop AIDS.

COMPREHENSION

Each sentence is false. Change the underlined word to make it true.

1. <u>All</u> of Keith Haring's art was just for fun.

2. The <u>scissors</u> in *Stop AIDS* symbolize "AIDS."

3. Haring made 20,000 <u>paintings</u> for people in South Africa in 1985.

■■■■■■■■■■■■■■■■■■■■■■■■■■■■■■■■■■■ *GO TO* MyEnglishLab *FOR MORE VOCABULARY PRACTICE.*

READING SKILL

1 Look at Reading Two on page 36. Circle the numbers. What information do these numbers give? Complete the chart to put the numbers in groups: order (first, second, third . . .), quantity (how many: 1, 2, 3 . . .), or date.

ORDER	QUANTITY	DATE
	two	

IDENTIFYING IMPORTANT NUMBERS

When you read, notice important numbers. Numbers will help you understand the reading.

– Ordinal numbers show order: first (1st), second (2nd), third (3rd), fourth (4th), fifth (5th)

– Cardinal numbers show quantity, or "how many": one (1), two (2), three (3)

– Dates (Years): 1964, 2015

    1964 = "nineteen sixty-four"
    2015 = "twenty fifteen"
    December 3, 1932 = "December third nineteen thirty-two"

Note that the number for the "day" (3) is written as a cardinal number but you say it as an ordinal number (third).

2 Look at the timeline on page 32 and Reading One on page 33. Underline the numbers. Then find two examples of numbers for order, quantity, or date. Write the sentences from the text.

Order

1. _____ *First, Haring liked to make art in public places, like in the subway.* _____

2. _____

Quantity

1. _____

2. _____

Date

1. _____

2. _____

GO TO MyEnglishLab *FOR MORE SKILL PRACTICE.*

STEP 1: Organize

Look at all of the Haring pictures in this unit again. What important ideas are in Haring's art? Check (✓) the boxes. Then share your answers with the class.

IDEAS IN HARING'S ART	RADIANT BABY	UNTITLED, 1984	FREE SOUTH AFRICA	STOP AIDS
POLITICS				
AIDS				
LOVE				
ENERGY				
FREEDOM				
CHILDREN				
OTHER: _____				

STEP 2: Synthesize

Use the chart in Step 1 to complete the sentences. Use each item only once.

1. _____ is about _____ and hope for the future. There are
   (picture)   (idea)
   rays around the child—like the rays of the sun. This shows the _____ of
                                                                        (idea)
   the child.

2. _____ shows how people can work together to end a serious problem
   (picture)
   such as _____.
             (idea)

3. In _____ you see a person. The person's arms go through his heart and
       (picture)
   brain. This picture shows how _____ is difficult.
                                       (idea)

4. _____ is about _____ .This picture is about the fight for
   (picture)   (idea)
   _____ in a country.
   (idea)

GO TO MyEnglishLab TO CHECK WHAT YOU LEARNED.

VOCABULARY

REVIEW

Complete the crossword puzzle with the words from the box on page 41.

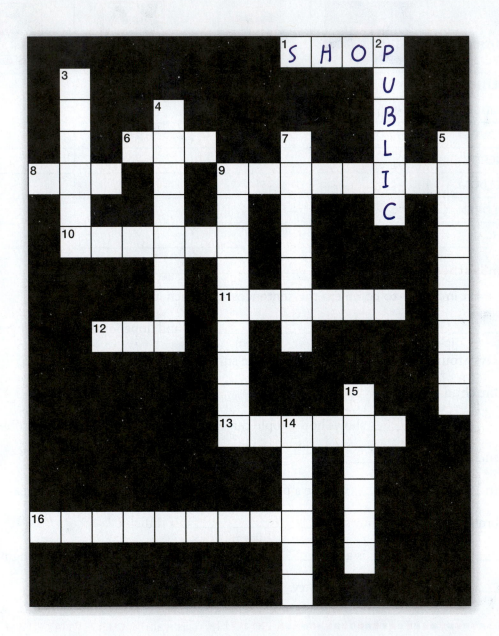

ads	famous	painter	sculpture
art	galleries	pop	~~shop~~
different	graffiti	poster	social
drawings	museum	~~public~~	symbol
energy			

Across

1. In 1988, Haring opened the Pop _____ in Tokyo. It closed in 1989.

6. He believed "_____ is for everyone."

8. The word _____ is short for "popular."

9. Some people said, "That is not art. It's just _____."

10. _____ issues were very important to Haring.

11. Haring had a lot of _____. You can see it in his art. It "moves."

12. The word _____ is short for "advertisements."

13. A wedding ring is a _____ of marriage.

16. A _____ is a work of art made of materials such as metal, stone, or wood.

Down

2. Haring made _____ art. He wanted everyone to see it.

3. People around the world know Haring. He is a _____ artist.

4. Someone who draws makes _____.

5. Haring was _____ from other artists.

7. A person who paints is a _____.

9. By the mid-1980s, Haring's work was in many art _____ around the world.

14. *El Prado* is a famous _____ in Madrid, Spain.

15. When I was a teenager, I had a *Happy Baby* _____ on my bedroom wall.

1 Study the two charts. The vocabulary from the unit is in bold.

NOUNS	ADJECTIVES	VERBS
dance dancer dancing	X	dance
drawing	X	draw
energy	energetic	energize
freedom	free	free
paint **painting** painter	X	paint
politics politician	political	X
poster post	posted	post
the public	**public**	publicize
sculpture sculptor sculpting	X	sculpt
symbol (of)	X	symbolize

A **noun** names:

a **person** (an artist, Pablo Picasso)
a **place** (a museum, London)
a **thing** (a drawing)
an **idea** (freedom) or **activity** (dancing)

Nouns for people end in -*ist*, -*er*, -*or*, or -*ian*

Painting and *drawing* have two meanings. One is a **thing** (count noun) and one is an **activity** (non-count noun).

Note: A singular count noun usually has a word like *a*, *an*, or *the* before it.

A **person** who paints is called a **painter** or an **artist**. But a person who draws is only called an **artist**, not a "**drawer**."

Thing: The *Mona Lisa* is a famous **painting**. My son made a **drawing** in his art class.

Activity: **Painting** is a popular hobby. She likes **drawing** pictures in art class.

A baby in Haring's art is **a** symbol of life.

The man in **the** photo is Andy Warhol.

An **adjective** describes a noun.	a **large** picture
	a **famous** person
Some adjectives, like *energetic*, *artistic*, and *public*, end in *-ic*.	
Most **verbs** show action.	Sofia **paints** very well.
	She **draws** well, too.
Other verbs like *be*, *have*, and *like* do not show action.	Sofia **is** from Australia.
	She **has** a sister and a brother.
	She **likes** to practice yoga.

2 Complete the sentences with the correct form of the words.

1. **(dance / dancing / dancer)**
   The tango is a _____ from Argentina.
   Julio Bocca is a famous tango _____ from Argentina.
   Bocca's _____ is beautiful.

2. **(draw / drawing)**
   This is a good _____ of my father. It looks like him.
   We _____ every day in art class.
   Children enjoy _____ in school.

3. **(energetic / energy / energize)**
   Patrick is too tired to dance. He has no _____.
   A cup of coffee will _____ him.
   If he sleeps well tonight, he will be more _____ tomorrow.

4. **(free / freedom)**
   In this country, people are _____ to say almost anything.
   Not every country has this _____.

5. **(paint / painter / painting)**
   I have to buy more _____ at the art store.
   I want to finish this _____. It's a picture of my house.
   _____ is a fun activity.
   I'm a good _____.

(continued on next page)

6. **(political / politics / politicians)**

I am not interested in _____.

My teacher's ideas are very _____.

Many _____ are honest, but some are not.

7. **(post / posts / posters)**

My sister has five _____ of her favorite movie actor on her bedroom wall.

My friends _____ photos of their vacations on Facebook®.

I like to read the _____ on your blog. You are a good writer.

8. **(public / the public / publicize)**

_____ likes the new show at the Shafrazi Gallery very much.

They _____ the big art shows on TV and in newspapers.

Mila likes to go to _____ places like parks and shopping malls.

9. **(sculptor / sculpture / sculpting)**

Constantin Brancusi is a famous _____.

"The Kiss" is a _____ by Brancusi.

_____ was one way he made art.

10. **(symbol / symbolizes)**

The color red _____ both "stop" and "love."

A red ribbon is a _____ of AIDS awareness.

CREATE

3 Write three more sentences about Keith Haring and his art. Use one word from the chart on page 42 in each sentence.

1. _____

2. _____

3. _____

GO TO MyEnglishLab FOR MORE VOCABULARY PRACTICE.

GRAMMAR

1 Read the information about Keith Haring. Then answer the questions.

AW: Was Haring different from other artists?

ER: Yes, he was.

AW: How was he different?

ER: Haring liked to make art in public places, like in the subway. He believed "art is for everyone." First, he was famous for his public art. Later, he became famous in galleries and museums. He was also different because magazines had ads with his paintings and drawings. His drawings were also on other things, such as Swatch watches. He also sold his art in the Pop Shop. He used his art in unusual ways to communicate with the world.

2 Underline *was, were,* and *had* in the interview above. How many examples can you find?

was _____   *were* _____   *had* _____

When do we use *am, is, are,* and *have*? _____

When do we use *was, were,* and *had*? _____

THE SIMPLE PAST OF *BE*

1. The simple past forms of *be* are *was* and *were*.	Keith Haring **was** an artist. Social issues **were** important to him.
2. For negative sentences use: subject + *was / were* + *not* In speaking and informal writing, use *wasn't / weren't*.	His art **was not** in museums in the early 1980s. His parents **were not** famous. His art **wasn't** in museums in the early 1980s. His parents **weren't** famous.

3. For *yes / no* questions, use:
was / were + subject
	Was Haring different from other artists?
	    Yes, he was.
	Were his drawings popular?
	    Yes, they were.
	Was Haring famous in the 1970s?
	    No, he wasn't.

4. For *Wh-* questions, use: *Wh-* word + *was / were* + subject	**Who was** Keith Haring? **What was** his art about? **How were** his pictures different?

THE SIMPLE PAST OF *HAVE*

1. The simple past form of *have* is *had*.	Haring **had** a lot of energy.
2. For negative sentences, use: *did* + *not* + *have* In speaking and informal writing, use: *didn't have*	Haring **did not have** a brother. Haring **didn't have** a brother.

3. For *yes / no* questions, use:
did + subject + *have*
	Did Haring have fun with his art?
	    Yes, he did.
	Did Haring have a long career?
	    No, he didn't.

4. For *Wh-* questions, use: *Wh-* word + *did* + subject + *have*	**Where did Haring have** fun? **When did Haring have** the most success?

3 Complete each sentence with *was, wasn't, were, weren't, had,* or *didn't have*.

1. Keith Haring and Andy Warhol _____*were*_____ famous artists in the 1980s.

2. Both Haring and Warhol _____ from Pennsylvania, but they _____ from different cities.

3. Haring and Warhol (not) _____ the same age. Warhol _____ 31 years older than Haring.

4. Warhol and Haring _____ a lot of friends.

5. Warhol _____ a student at the Carnegie Institute of Technology.

6. In the 1950s, Warhol _____ a job on Madison Avenue in New York.

7. He _____ an artist for *Vogue* and *Glamour* magazines.

8. He (not) _____ a lot of money at that time.

9. By the early 1960s, Andy Warhol _____ a famous Pop artist.

10. Like Haring's art, Warhol's art _____ controversial.

11. Warhol _____ a painter, sculptor, writer, and filmmaker.

12. Keith Haring _____ a painter and a sculptor, but he (not) _____ a writer or a filmmaker.

13. Warhol and Haring _____ good friends in the 1980s.

14. Haring _____ very sad when Warhol died in 1987.

15. Warhol _____ 58 years old when he died.

16. He (not) _____ a very long life.

4 Work with a partner. Write questions about Keith Haring and his art. Use the past forms of *be* and *have*.

1. Who / be / Keith Haring? <u>Who was Keith Haring?</u>

2. Be / Haring / famous in the 1970s? _____

3. Be / Keith Haring / energetic? _____

4. In what city / be / Haring / born? _____

5. Be / Haring / only a painter? _____

6. Why / be / his art / controversial? _____

7. Be / the Pop Shop / a restaurant? _____

8. Where / be / the two Pop Shops? _____

9. How old / be / Keith Haring / in 1990? _____

5 Give your book to your partner. Your partner will write answers to your questions in full sentences.

Your partner's answers:

1. <u>Keith Haring was an artist in the 1980s.</u>

2. _____

3. _____

4. _____

5. _____

6. _____

7. _____

8. _____

9. _____

GO TO MyEnglishLab *FOR MORE GRAMMAR PRACTICE AND TO CHECK WHAT YOU LEARNED.*

FINAL WRITING TASK

In this unit, you read a timeline and an interview about Keith Haring. You also looked at examples of Keith Haring's art.

You are going to **write a biography paragraph about Keith Haring**. A biography is a story of a person's life. Use the grammar and vocabulary from the unit.*

PREPARE TO WRITE: Finding Information in a Reading

To help you plan your biography, you are going to **look for information in the readings** in this unit as a prewriting activity.

1 Look at the timeline on page 32. Then answer the questions about Keith Haring.

1. Where was Keith Haring born?

   Keith Haring was born in Kutztown, Pennsylvania.

2. When was Keith Haring born?

   _____

3. When was Haring arrested by the police? Why?

   _____

4. When and where was Haring an art student?

   _____

5. What were his first drawings? Where were they?

   _____

6. When and where was Haring's first important art show?

   _____

---

* For Alternative Writing Topics, see page 53. These topics can be used in place of the writing topic for this unit or as homework. The alternative topics relate to the theme of the unit, but may not target the same grammar or rhetorical structures taught in the unit.

2 Look at Reading One on page 33. Find one more idea about Keith Haring that you think is interesting. Write it on the line. Use this information in your biography, too.

_____

WRITE: Time Order

A biography usually gives events in **time order** (in the order they happened). The writer begins with the first event and ends with the last event.

1 Read the sentences about Andy Warhol. Number the sentences in time order from **1** to **7**.

_____ **a.** Warhol was a student at Carnegie Institute of Technology from 1945 to 1949.

_____ **b.** Andy Warhol and Keith Haring were good friends in the 1980s.

_____ **c.** Andy Warhol died in 1987.

_____ **d.** By the early 1960s, Andy Warhol was a famous Pop artist.

___1___ **e.** Andy Warhol was born in Pennsylvania in 1912.

_____ **f.** In the 1950s, Warhol was a commercial artist[1] on Madison Avenue in New York.

_____ **g.** Then Warhol had his first art show in 1952.

2 Work with a partner. Compare your answers for Exercise 1. Were your answers the same as your partner's? Talk about any differences.

3 Look at your answers to the questions about Keith Haring in Prepare to Write on page 49. Put them in time order.

4 Write your first draft. Include a topic sentence that gives the main idea of your paragraph. Write sentences to explain or support the main idea. Don't worry about grammar yet. Just try to make your ideas clear.

_____

[1] **commercial artist:** an artist who works for an advertising company for business or money

Using commas correctly makes your writing clearer and easier to understand.

1 Study the chart.

USING COMMAS	
Use commas:	
in complete dates between the day and the year.	Keith Haring was born on May 4, 1958.
between a city and country or state.	The Harings were from Kutztown, Pennsylvania. Haring visited Madrid, Spain.
after the city *and* country (or state) name *when* there are more words after the country / state.	They lived in Kutztown, Pennsylvania, in the 1970s. Haring visited Madrid, Spain, many times.
Do not use commas:	
if the month and year are separated by a preposition.	Haring was born in May **of** 1958.
if the city and country (or state) names are separated by more information.	Kutztown **is in the state of** Pennsylvania.
if the city, state, country, name of the month, or year is used alone.	The Harings were from Kutztown. Haring lived in Pennsylvania when he was young. Haring visited Spain many times. Haring was born in May. He was born in 1958.

2 Add commas to these sentences. Not every sentence needs commas.

1. Haring was born on May 4 1958.

2. Haring moved to New York New York in 1978.

3. He had his first important show in 1982.

4. Haring opened The Pop Shop in New York City in 1986. It closed in September of 1995.

5. The Pop Shop in Tokyo Japan opened on January 30 1988. It closed in 1989.

6. Haring died on Friday February 16 1990.

3 Write three sentences about yourself (for example, your address or your birthday). Use commas correctly.

1. _____

2. _____

3. _____

GO TO MyEnglishLab *FOR MORE SKILL PRACTICE.*

EDIT: Writing the Final Draft

Go to MYENGLISHLAB and write the final draft of your paragraph. Check your grammar, spelling, capitalization, and punctuation. Check that you used some of the grammar and vocabulary from the unit. Use the checklist to help you write your final draft. Then give your paragraph to your teacher.

FINAL DRAFT CHECKLIST

❏ Did you use a capital letter at the beginning of each sentence?

❏ Did you use a period at the end of each sentence?

❏ Did you use the past forms of *be* and *have*?

❏ Did you use commas in the correct places?

❏ Did you use vocabulary from the unit?

❏ Did you put the events in time order?

UNIT PROJECT

Work alone or with a partner. Follow these steps:

STEP 1: Go to the website of the Keith Haring Foundation: www.haring.com. Spend some time looking at the website.

STEP 2: Click on "Art." Look at Keith Haring's art from year to year.

STEP 3: Choose one piece of art. Write about it. What do you see? What is it about? Why do you like it?

STEP 4: Present your piece of art to the class. Talk about it. Your classmates will ask you questions about it.

ALTERNATIVE WRITING TOPICS

Write about one of the topics. Use the vocabulary and grammar from the unit.

1. Look again at the pictures on pages 33 and 36. Choose one picture. Write five to ten sentences about this picture. What do you see? What is it about? How does it make you feel?

2. Keith Haring used simple symbols (such as babies, dogs, and dancers) that were important to people in the 1970s and 1980s. What symbols are important to people today? Draw one. Write five to ten sentences about your symbol.

3. Keith Haring wanted everyone to experience his art. It was "art for everyone." What do you think? Was Haring's art "for everyone"? Write five to ten sentences.

4. Haring's art was controversial, especially in the 1980s. Some people liked it, and some people didn't like it. Look again at the pictures on pages 33 and 36. Why do you think Haring's art was controversial? Write five to ten sentences about Haring and his art.

GO TO MyEnglishLab TO WRITE ABOUT ONE OF THE ALTERNATIVE TOPICS, WATCH A VIDEO ABOUT ART, AND TAKE THE UNIT 2 ACHIEVEMENT TEST.

WHAT'S IT WORTH TO You?

1 FOCUS ON THE TOPIC

1. What does the man have?

2. Why does he have so many?

3. What other things do people keep?

GO TO MyEnglishLab *TO CHECK WHAT YOU KNOW.*

VOCABULARY

Read the passage. Then write the boldfaced word next to its definition on the next page. Compare your answers with a partner's.

ANTIQUES ROADSHOW

Antiques Roadshow is a popular television show. The show travels to different cities. The **guests** are regular people. They bring their special possessions to the show. They tell stories and ask questions.

The guests bring many kinds of **items**. Some guests bring antiques—old and **valuable** things, such as art, furniture, or jewelry. Other guests bring **collections** of many toys or books. Some items are very common and are not **worth** a lot of money. But others are very valuable. Some of the items are in very bad **condition**, but others are in great condition— just like new. Some items have only **sentimental** value—maybe the item was a gift from someone special or brings back good memories. Maybe it is just an item you like a lot—a **favorite** item.

Antiques **experts** give information about the items. The experts also say how much the items are worth. The guests always want to know the value of their items.

People can learn a lot on this show. This type of TV show started in England more than 20 years ago. You can see shows like it in other countries around the world.

---

[1] **secret:** information that you don't tell other people

_____ 1. people with a lot of knowledge and experience with something

_____ 2. people who visit a person or place

_____ 3. having a value in personal feelings or emotions

_____ 4. objects or things

_____ 5. the physical state of something—good or bad

_____ 6. having a high price, worth a lot of money

_____ 7. groups of things that people like to keep

_____ 8. equal to, in money

_____ 9. being liked more than others

GO TO MyEnglishLab *FOR MORE VOCABULARY PRACTICE.*

PREVIEW

Dan Stone writes a sports column for the *Boston Daily News*. Read the beginning of the sports column. Then, with a partner, answer the question: What is Dan Stone's secret?

My Secret

by **Dan Stone**

I am a sports writer, and I love my job because I love sports. But I have a little secret.

Every Monday night I watch my favorite TV show. If the telephone rings, I don't answer it. I tell my friends that I am watching *Monday Night Football*, but that isn't true.

Now read Dan Stone's column on the next page.

My Secret

by Dan Stone

1   I am a sports writer, and I love my job because I love sports. But I have a little secret.

2   Every Monday night I watch my **favorite** TV show. If the telephone rings, I don't answer it. I tell my friends that I am watching *Monday Night Football*, but that isn't true.

3   Sometimes my favorite show is more exciting than *Monday Night Football*. Here is my secret: On Monday nights I watch *Antiques Roadshow*. It is a show about antiques and **collections**. Fourteen million people watch it every week.

4   The show is simple. The **guests** on the show are real people. The guests bring in old art, furniture, books, toys, and more. First, the guests tell the **experts** about their **items**. Then the experts talk about the items. Finally, the experts say how much the items are **worth**. You get a lot of information.

5   One woman, Veronica, had an old painting. Veronica's grandmother got the picture for free in 1925. The expert looked at Veronica's picture carefully and said, "Thomas Cole is the artist. Cole painted this around 1835. Your painting is worth about $125,000." Veronica was very surprised. She told the expert, "Wow! That's a lot of money! But I don't care about the money. The painting has a lot of **sentimental** value."

6   I want *Antiques Roadshow* to visit my city. I can't wait! I have a baseball signed by Babe Ruth and Jackie Robinson in the 1940s. It's in perfect **condition**. I also have a baseball card collection. I keep it in a box under my bed. The ball and the cards have sentimental value. My father gave them to me. But I don't really like to play or watch baseball. Maybe they're worth a lot of money!

7   And you? Are you ready? Look carefully around your home! You might have something very **valuable**.

MAIN IDEAS

1 Look again at your prediction in the Preview section on page 57. Was your prediction correct?

2 Read each sentence. Check (✓) **True** or **False**. Then write the number of the paragraph where you found the answer.

	True	False	Paragraph Number
1. People who watch *Antiques Roadshow* can learn a lot.	❏	❏	_____
2. Dan Stone watches football on Monday nights.	❏	❏	_____
3. *Antiques Roadshow* is a sports show.	❏	❏	_____
4. *Antiques Roadshow* buys items from the guests.	❏	❏	_____

DETAILS

Match each question to the correct answer. Then write the number of the paragraph where you found the answer.

___c___ **1.** What do Stone's friends think he watches on Monday nights?   __2__

_____ **2.** How many people watch *Antiques Roadshow* every week?   _____

_____ **3.** What do people bring to *Antiques Roadshow*?   _____

_____ **4.** How much is the woman's painting worth?   _____

_____ **5.** What items does Stone have from his father?   _____

    a. items from home   **d.** a signed baseball and his baseball cards

    b. $125,000   **e.** 14 million

    ~~**c.** football~~

MAKE INFERENCES

INFERRING OUTCOMES

An **inference** is **an "educated" guess** about something. The information is **not stated directly** in the reading. Good readers put ideas together to find the answer. Writers don't always say what will happen next. A reader can make an inference, or guess the outcome. Inferring an outcome can help you better understand what you read.

Look at the example. Check **probably yes** or **probably no**. Then read the explanation.

Veronica will sell her painting.

_____ probably yes

_____ probably no

The best answer is *probably no*. How do we know?

In paragraph 6, we learn the painting is worth $125,000. Veronica says, "That's a lot of money! But I don't care about the money. The painting has a lot of sentimental value."

We know Veronica does not care about the money. We know the painting has sentimental value. We understand that, for Veronica, the money isn't important. After reading closely, we can guess that Veronica will not sell her painting.

1 Read each sentence. Check (✓) **probably yes** or **probably no**. Look at the numbered paragraphs to help you find the answers.

1. Dan's friends will laugh at him if they learn his secret. (paragraph 2)

   _____ probably yes
   _____ probably no

2. Dan will take his signed baseball and his baseball cards to *Antiques Roadshow*. (paragraph 6)

   _____ probably yes
   _____ probably no

3. Dan will sell his signed baseball and his baseball cards. (paragraph 6)

   _____ probably yes
   _____ probably no

2 Share your answers with a partner. Point to sentences that helped you find the answers.

EXPRESS OPINIONS

In his column, Dan Stone said, "Fourteen million people watch it every week." Why is *Antiques Roadshow* popular? Check (✓) all the possible answers. Then share your answers with the class.

Antiques Roadshow is popular because _____.

_____ **1.** people like learning

_____ **2.** people need money

_____ **3.** the people on the show are funny

_____ **4.** people remember their family's past

_____ **5.** the items are interesting

_____ **6.** the guests are real people

_____ **7.** your idea: _____.

▪▪▪▪▪▪▪▪▪▪▪▪▪▪▪▪▪▪▪▪▪▪▪▪ *GO TO* MyEnglishLab *TO GIVE YOUR OPINION ABOUT ANOTHER QUESTION.*

READING TWO BE A SMART COLLECTOR

READ

1 Look at the boldfaced words in the reading on the next page and think about the questions.

1. Which of these words do you know?

2. What do the words mean?

2 Read the rules from an expert about collecting.

BE A SMART COLLECTOR

Starting a collection is easy, but be a smart collector. Here are four rules:

RULE 1: Enjoy. Collect things that you are interested in. Collect things that you want to keep for a long time.

RULE 2: Learn. Become an expert. Read a lot. Talk to antiques experts. Ask a lot of questions. Don't worry! Experts love to talk.

RULE 3: Look for the best. Collect things in good condition. For example, an antique toy in "mint," or perfect, condition will be valuable in the future. A **similar** toy in bad condition will not be as valuable.

RULE 4: Collect **rare** items. Rare things are more valuable than common things. If the items you collect are rare today, they will be more valuable in the future.

COMPREHENSION

Match each example with one of the rules in the reading. Write the rule number (**1, 2, 3,** or **4**) on the line.

A ripped stamp

_____ **a.** First, learn about antique toys. Then collect them.

_____ **b.** Collecting coins from the 1800s is better than collecting common coins from today.

_____ **c.** If you love Barbie® dolls, then collect them.

_____ **d.** Don't buy a stamp for your collection if it is ripped.

GO TO MyEnglishLab FOR MORE VOCABULARY PRACTICE.

READING SKILL

1 Look at Rule 1 from Reading Two again. In Rule 1, the writer wants the reader to do three things. What are they? Underline the writer's three suggestions.

IDENTIFYING SUGGESTIONS

When you read, it's important to notice when the writer wants you to do something. Writers often use commands, called **imperatives**, to make suggestions.

In Unit 1, you learned that a sentence has a subject and a verb. **Imperatives** are the base form of the verb without a subject. The subject is not written, but we understand that the subject is *you*.

Understood Subject

Subject	Verb
(You)	Enjoy.
(You)	Collect things that you are interested in.
(You)	Collect things that you want to keep for a long time.

These are the writer's three suggestions in Rule 1.

2 Look at Rules 2, 3, and 4 in Reading Two. Underline the suggestions.

■■■■■■■■■■■■■■■■■■■■■■■■■■■■■■■■■ *GO TO* MyEnglishLab *FOR MORE SKILL PRACTICE.*

CONNECT THE READINGS

STEP 1: Organize

Read Dan Stone's column again. How does Dan follow the four rules? Match the ideas about Dan's collection with the rules for collecting on page 62.

	IDEAS FROM DAN STONE'S COLUMN
RULE 1: ENJOY _____	a. The baseball is rare. It was signed by two famous baseball players.
RULE 2: LEARN _____	b. His baseball is in perfect condition.
RULE 3: LOOK FOR THE BEST _____	c. He watches *Antiques Roadshow*.
RULE 4: COLLECT RARE ITEMS _____	d. Dan doesn't like baseball, but his signed baseball has sentimental value.

(continued on next page)

STEP 2: Synthesize

Dan Stone has a collection of baseball items. Is Dan Stone a smart collector? Did he follow the four rules? Complete the first sentence. Then write 4–5 more sentences to explain.

Dan Stone (is / isn't) a smart collector. He _____

_____

_____

_____

_____

GO TO MyEnglishLab *TO CHECK WHAT YOU LEARNED.*

3 FOCUS ON WRITING

VOCABULARY

REVIEW

Complete the sentences with the correct words.

1. **(condition / valuable)**

   I found some of my childhood toys in my mother's house. Maybe they are _____ today. They are all in good _____.

2. **(guest / worth)**

   My mother wants to be a _____ on *Antiques Roadshow*. She wants to bring her antique watch. The watch isn't _____ very much, but she enjoys wearing it.

3. **(collection / collector / collect)**

   I began to _____ stamps when I was ten years old. I plan to give my _____ to my son when he is ten years old. I hope he wants to be a stamp _____ like me.

4. (sentimental / rare / similar)

This was my grandparents' kitchen table. It is very _____, so you can't buy a _____ table today. It isn't a beautiful table, but I keep it because it has a lot of _____ value.

5. (expert / items / favorite)

My father likes to read about the past. His _____ subject is the U.S. Civil War. He is an _____ on the Civil War. He knows a lot about it, and he collects _____ from the war.

EXPAND

Remember that a **noun** names a person, place, thing, or idea. An **adjective** is a word that describes a noun. A **verb** is a word that shows an action.

Many nouns end in *-tion, -ment, -ity,* and *-or.* Many adjectives end in *-ing, -ed, -al, -able,* and *-ible.*

Many words such as *expert* and *sports* are both a noun and an adjective.

Work with a partner. In your notebook, make a chart like the one below. Put the words into the correct group.

collect	collector	excited	~~expert~~	similar	valuable
collectible	condition	excitement	possession	similarity	value
collection	excite	exciting	sentimental	sports	

NOUNS	ADJECTIVES	VERBS
expert	expert	

CREATE

Write your special possession or collection on the first line. Then write sentences about it. Use one word from the Expand section in each sentence.

Example

My special possession is a watch. It is valuable.

1. _____

2. _____

3. _____

4. _____

GO TO MyEnglishLab *FOR MORE VOCABULARY PRACTICE.*

GRAMMAR

1 Read the excerpt from "My Secret." Then answer the questions.

> I am a sports writer, and I love my job because I love sports. But I have a little secret.
> Every Monday night I watch my favorite TV show. If the telephone rings, I don't answer it. I tell my friends that I am watching *Monday Night Football*, but that isn't true.

1. How many verbs are there? Underline them.

2. Which verbs are negative? Circle them.

3. These sentences are about _____.

    a. the past   **b.** the present   **c.** the future

THE SIMPLE PRESENT	
1. Use the **simple present** for everyday actions or facts.	I **have** a secret. If the telephone **rings**, I **don't answer** it.
2. When the subject is *he*, *she*, or *it*, put an *-s* at the end of the regular verbs. REMEMBER: *be* and *have* are irregular.	She collect**s** antique jewelry. *Antiques Roadshow* **is** my favorite show. Dan **has** a secret.
3. For negative sentences, use: *do* / *does* + *not* + **the base form of the verb** Use the contractions *don't* and *doesn't* in speaking and informal writing.	Dan **does not watch** football on Mondays. I **do not like** to play golf. If the telephone rings, I **don't** answer it.
4. For *yes* / *no* **questions**, use: *Do* / *Does* + subject + **the base form of the verb** Use *do* or *does* in short answers.	**Do diamonds cost** a lot? **Yes, they do.** **Does Dan Stone watch** football on Mondays? **No, he doesn't.**
5. For *wh-* **questions**, use: *Wh-* word + *do* / *does* + subject + **the base form of the verb**	**What do you watch** on Monday nights? **Where do you like** to play golf? **How much does that car cost?**

2 Complete the conversation with the simple present form of each verb.

EXPERT: Welcome to *Antiques Roadshow*. What _____do_____ you

_____have_____ with you today?
1. (have)

WOMAN: I _____ my mother's diamond wedding ring. I love this ring! I
2. (have)

_____ my mother when I _____ it.
3. (remember)   4. (wear)

EXPERT: _____ you _____ it often?
5. (wear)

WOMAN: Yes, I _____. I never _____ it off.
6. (do)   7. (take)

EXPERT: What _____ you _____ about this ring?
8. (know)

WOMAN: My father gave it to my mother in 1964. I _____ where he got it.
9. (not / know)

My husband _____ that it _____ worth a lot
10. (not / think)   11. (be)

of money. _____ it _____ valuable to you?
12. (look)

EXPERT: Well, it _____ a beautiful ring, but I have some bad news. This
13. (be)

_____ a real diamond. It _____ fake. It is
14. (not / be)   15. (be)

worth about $50.

WOMAN: Really? My husband was right! Well, I still _____ it.
16. (love)

My husband and I _____ to give it to our daughter. We
17. (plan)

_____ this ring to stay in our family. It _____
18. (want)   19. (have)

a lot of sentimental value. Thank you very much!

■■■■■■■■■■■ **GO TO** MyEnglishLab **FOR MORE GRAMMAR PRACTICE AND TO CHECK WHAT YOU LEARNED.**

FINAL WRITING TASK

In this unit, you read about special possessions and collections. Now you are going to *write a paragraph about your own special possession or collection*. Use the vocabulary and grammar from the unit.*

PREPARE TO WRITE: Asking Yourself Questions

To get ideas for your writing, you are going to **ask yourself questions** about a topic. For example: Do I have a special possession or collection? What is it? Why do I keep it? Was it a gift? Does it have sentimental value? Is it worth a lot of money?

1 Think of some special possessions or collections that you have. Make a list of four or five items. A special possession can be something that:

- you collect.
- you received as a gift.
- helps you remember a special person, event, or time in your life.

Example

My Special Possessions:

my high school soccer shirt   *my grandfather's painting*   *family photos*

2 Choose two special possessions from the list you made. Complete the chart.

	POSSESSION 1	POSSESSION 2
1. What is your special possession?		
2. Where did you get it?		
3. How much is it worth?		
4. Why do you keep it?		

3 Choose one possession to write about.

WRITE: A Paragraph

Remember that a **paragraph** is a group of sentences about one main idea. The first sentence usually gives the main idea of the paragraph. It is called the topic sentence. The other sentences explain or support the topic sentence.

---

* For Alternative Writing Topics, see page 73. These topics can be used in place of the writing topic for this unit or as homework. The alternative topics relate to the theme of the unit, but may not target the same grammar or rhetorical structures taught in the unit.

1 Read the paragraph. Then answer the questions.

Left margin →

Indent →

Right margin

> Antiques experts like to be on Antiques Roadshow because it is good for their business. They do not receive any money from the TV show, but they become famous. People watching TV learn the names of the experts. They also learn the names of the experts' companies. The experts get more business if they are on Antiques Roadshow.

1. What is the main idea of this paragraph? Circle the sentence that has the main idea.

2. Does the writer begin each new sentence on a new line, or does the writer continue on the same line?

3. When does the writer stop and move down to the next line?

2 Write two paragraphs with these sentences on a separate piece of paper. The sentences are in the correct order. Follow the rules for paragraph form. Your paragraphs will look like the paragraph in Exercise 1.

Sentences for Paragraph 1

One day, a man named Russ Pritchard was a guest on *Antiques Roadshow*.

He had a large sword.

When he was young, Pritchard found the sword in his new house.

George Juno, an antiques expert, told Pritchard it was an American Civil War sword.

Juno said the sword was very rare and worth $35,000.

Pritchard was very surprised to hear this.

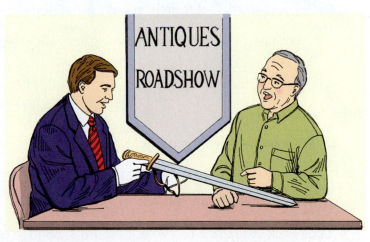

(continued on next page)

Sentences for Paragraph 2

Two years later, there was a story in the newspaper about Pritchard and Juno.

WGBH, a Boston TV station, learned that Pritchard's story was not true.

Pritchard and Juno made up the story together.

WGBH was very angry because it wants only true stories on *Antiques Roadshow*.

As a result, Juno cannot be on *Antiques Roadshow* in the future.

3 Read the paragraph. Underline the topic sentence.

One of my special possessions is my collection of family photographs. I have hundreds of photos. I have very old photos of my great-grandparents. I also have pictures of my grandparents' wedding. I especially love the photos of my parents when they were children. Sometimes I spend hours looking at the pictures. I like the photos because my family is very important to me.

4 Read the paragraph. It is missing a topic sentence. Read the topic sentences. Choose the best topic sentence and write it on the line.

_____. It is yellow and black and has the number "11" on it. It also has my name on the back. I got it in high school when I played on the school's team. Our team won every game. The shirt has a lot of sentimental value. I keep it because I like to remember those games and my teammates. We had a lot of fun together.

Topic Sentences

a. My team won every game in high school.

b. My high school soccer shirt is very important to me.

c. Soccer is my favorite sport.

5 Look back at Prepare to Write, Exercise 3, on page 68. What special possession are you going to write about? Write a topic sentence for your paragraph.

6 Now write your first draft about your special possession. Include a topic sentence that gives the main idea of your paragraph. Write sentences to explain or support the main idea. Don't worry about grammar yet. Just try to make your ideas clear.

REVISE: Staying on the Topic

All the sentences in a paragraph explain and support the main idea. Sentences about other ideas or topics do not belong. Read the paragraph. The topic sentence is underlined. One sentence is not about the main idea. It is crossed out.

One of my special possessions is a painting by my grandfather. He was not a professional painter, but he painted as a hobby. ~~My sister also paints.~~ My favorite painting is a picture of the house where my father grew up. The house is yellow, and there are trees around it. My grandfather gave me the picture before he died. I think of him when I look at the picture.

1 Read the paragraph. Underline the topic sentence. Cross out one sentence that is not about the main idea. Work with a partner. Explain why you chose that sentence to cross out.

My bicycle is a very special possession. My bike is not worth a lot of money. It is old, but it is in good condition. I ride my bike every day. I ride it to school, to the store, and to my grandmother's house. I walk to these places in the summer. I can go wherever I want because I have a bike.

2 Look at the first draft of your paragraph. Do all the sentences explain and support the topic sentence? Cross out the sentences that are not about the main idea. If necessary, write new sentences.

■■■■■■■■■■■■■■■■■■■■■■■■■■■■■■■■ **GO TO** MyEnglishLab **FOR MORE SKILL PRACTICE.**

EDIT: Writing the Final Draft

Go to MYENGLISHLAB and write the final draft of your paragraph. Check your grammar, spelling, capitalization, and punctuation. Check that you used some of the grammar and vocabulary from the unit. Use the checklist to help you write your final draft. Then give your paragraph to your teacher.

UNIT PROJECT

Many collectors buy and sell antiques online. They use websites like the Internet Antiques Shop (www.TIAS.com), Junkables (www.junkables.com), or Ebay (www.ebay.com).

Other collectors buy and sell antiques in stores. A **thrift shop** is a store that sells old things at a cheap price. An **antiques store** also has old things, but the things at an antiques store are rarer and more expensive.

Write about an antique or collectible item. Follow these steps:

STEP 1: Go to one of these websites for antiques and collectibles. Choose one item on the website. Read about the item. You can also visit a thrift shop or an antiques store. Choose one item in the store and learn about the item. Then write answers to these questions:

- What is it?

- How old is it?

- What does it look like?

- Is it valuable? Why or why not?

STEP 2: Write a paragraph about the item. Use some of your answers to the questions from Step 1. Start your paragraph like this: "I learned about an interesting antique (or collectible) item."

STEP 3: Share your writing with a partner. Read your partner's paragraph. Then answer these questions:

- Did the writer indent the first line of the paragraph?

- Did the writer use margins correctly?

- Which sentences explain why the item is interesting? Underline them.

ALTERNATIVE WRITING TOPICS

Write about one of the topics. Use the vocabulary and grammar from the unit.

1. Ask someone about his or her favorite possession or collection. Write a paragraph about the person's answer.

2. Why do people bring items to *Antiques Roadshow*? Are they interested in history and sentimental value? Are they interested in money? Write a paragraph with your opinion.

3. Is there a TV show like *Antiques Roadshow* in your country? If yes, write a paragraph about the show.

GO TO MyEnglishLab *TO WRITE ABOUT ONE OF THE ALTERNATIVE TOPICS, WATCH A VIDEO ABOUT A STOLEN WEDDING DRESS, AND TAKE THE UNIT 3 ACHIEVEMENT TEST.*

OPEN FOR
Business

1 FOCUS ON THE TOPIC

1. What do you see in the picture?

2. What can a person do at this place?

3. Do you like big stores like this? Why or why not?

GO TO MyEnglishLab TO CHECK WHAT YOU KNOW.

VOCABULARY

1 Read the list of words and their definitions.

customer: a person who buys things in a store; a shopper

price: the money that you pay to buy something

employee: a person who works in a store or business

products: things a person makes and sells

own: to have something that is yours

service: work that someone does for you

owner: someone who owns something

shop: go to a store in order to buy things; a small store

personal attention: special help or service that someone gives you

shopping: the activity of going to stores to buy things

2 Complete the text with words from the list.

customers	~~own~~	personal attention	products	shop
employees	owner	prices	service	shopping

I'm Alexander Ree, and I _____own_____ Ree's Menswear.
                                    1.

At Ree's Menswear, we care about you, our _____.
                                                          2.

We give _____ to every customer who visits our
                  3.

store. Our _____ always give friendly
                      4.

_____ so you feel happy in our _____.
          5.   6.

We have good _____, so you save money.
                          7.

Most important, we make an excellent _____. When
                                                          8.

you buy something from Ree's Menswear, you will enjoy it for life.

I always say, "If you look bad, we look bad!"

Thank you for _____ at Ree's Menswear.
                          9.

Alexander Ree

Alexander Ree

_____ of Ree's Menswear
          10.

Visit us in one of our stores or visit us online at reesmenswear.com.

GO TO MyEnglishLab FOR MORE VOCABULARY PRACTICE.

PREVIEW

1 You are going to read an article about business. First, read about two different kinds of stores. Then complete the chart.

A **chain store** has many stores with the same name. 7-Eleven® and Starbucks® are chain stores. Large companies usually own chain stores. Some chain stores are called "big box" stores because they are very big and sell many different products. Wal-Mart® and IKEA® are examples of big-box chain stores.

A **locally-owned store** is smaller than a chain store. The owner usually lives in the community or not far away. Sometimes a locally-owned business is called a "mom and pop" store because a family owns it.

(continued on next page)

2 What are the benefits (good points) and drawbacks (bad points) of shopping at the two kinds of stores? Add your own ideas to the ideas in the chart.

LOCALLY-OWNED STORES		BIG-BOX STORES	
BENEFITS	**DRAWBACKS**	**BENEFITS**	**DRAWBACKS**
The service is good.	They don't have all the things I want.	They have more products.	The service isn't good.

3 Now read the online article.

E-Business Magazine
The Debate[1] Space: Mom & Pop vs. Big Box

1 **Today's debate topic:** Is it better to **shop** at mom and pop stores and not at big-box stores?

2 *Please Shop at a Mom and Pop!*
by Patty Sanders

3 Locally-owned stores are important for our community. We are in big trouble if we lose our small businesses—we need to keep them.

4 At mom and pop stores, **customers** feel like family. **Owners** and **employees** remember the regular customers and their families. They also know every **product**. They can talk to customers about the products. This **personal attention** makes the local community strong. We don't get this personal attention at big-box stores. Large chain stores often have more products and lower **prices** than smaller stores. But in the end, the personal attention is worth a few extra dollars.

5 How can our community live without small businesses? Large chain stores do not care about our families—we are not important to them. They care about making money. We can't lose our small stores. If the small businesses die, our community will die too!

---

[1]**debate:** two or more people giving different opinions about a topic

6 ***Big-Box Stores Aren't the Bad Guy***
by Butch Baker

7 The fact is: People need to save money so they will have it when they need it. Who cares about friendly **service**? People want low prices! So stop crying about personal attention! I don't believe it. Big-box stores have low prices because they sell more products. People want to save money. That's it!

8 **Shopping** at big-box stores is also more convenient. That is, big-box stores make life easier because they have more products. It's one-stop shopping. At my Wal-Mart® Supercenter I can get food, clothes, gas for my car, and much more. Why stop at five different stores if I can stop at just one? That's crazy.

9 Big-box stores are always less expensive and more convenient. People who say big-box stores are bad are totally wrong.

10 **READER COMMENTS:**

11 Not all mom and pop employees are friendly and helpful. And not all big-box stores are cold and impersonal. Both have benefits. —Caroline

12 National and international chain stores bring jobs to the community, but the pay is very low. Many families don't make enough money to live. —Albert Chow, CPA

13 I shop where the prices are low and the store hours are convenient. I'm too busy to worry about "mom and pop." —Mr. Mom

14 At Brooklyn Market we sell fresh food from local farms. We **own** a small store that helps our community. And the people in our community help each other. —Melissa and Gail

MAIN IDEAS

1 Look again at your predictions in the Preview section on page 78. Add information from the reading to the chart on page 78.

2 Which writer agrees with these statements? Write the sentences in the correct box on the next page.

- Customers care about good prices.
- It is important for employees to speak to customers and help them.
- Small businesses are important for the community.
- Large chain stores make life easier for customers.

PATTY SANDERS	BUTCH BAKER
• •	• •

DETAILS

Complete each sentence with a name from the reading.

Patty Sanders   Caroline   Mr. Mom
Butch Baker   Albert Chow   Melissa and Gail

1. _____ enjoys personal attention when she shops.

2. _____ is worried about employees' low pay at chain stores.

3. _____ isn't interested in personal attention when he shops.

4. _____ likes both locally-owned stores and big-box stores.

5. _____ own a store that sells food.

6. _____ doesn't have a lot of time to shop.

MAKE INFERENCES

INFERRING TONE

An **inference** is an **"educated" guess** about something. The information is **not stated directly** in the reading. Good readers put ideas together to find the answers. **Tone** shows emotion. When you speak, your friends know your emotions because of your words and the sound, or tone, of your voice. When you read, you must infer the tone because you can't hear the writer's voice.

A writer's "voice" can sound happy, angry, or worried. It can also sound *neutral* (no specific emotion).

Look at the example and answer the questions. Then read the explanation.

Reread "*Please Shop at a Mom and Pop!*" by Patty Sanders on page 78. What is the feeling or emotion in her words? Circle the best one.

a. angry
b. sad
c. happy
d. worried
e. confused

What words or phrases in the reading show this emotion? Underline them.

The best answer is *d*. Patty Sanders sounds worried. We know this because she uses words and phrases such as:

- We are in **big trouble** if we lose our small businesses.
- **How can our community live** without small businesses?
- We **can't lose** our small stores.
- If the small businesses die, our **community will die** too!

From these boldfaced words and phrases, we can infer that Patty Sanders' tone is worried.

1 Read Butch Baker's opinion in Reading One. What is his tone? Choose the best answer. Underline words or phrases in the reading that express his tone.

      a. angry

      b. sad

      c. happy

      d. worried

      e. confused

      f. neutral

2 Which writer uses a neutral tone? _____

      How do you know?_____

EXPRESS OPINIONS

Work in groups of three. Who do you agree with, Patty Sanders or Butch Baker? Discuss your ideas. Then complete at least one sentence.

- I prefer to shop at _____ because _____
- _____ is most important to me. I go to a store if _____
- I agree with _____. I think _____

■■■■■■■■■■■■■■■■■■■■■■■ *GO TO* MyEnglishLab *TO GIVE YOUR OPINION ABOUT ANOTHER QUESTION.*

READD

1 Look at the boldfaced words and phrases in the reading and think about the **questions.**

1. Which of these words do you know?

2. What do the words mean?

2 Read the online magazine article about Etsy, an Internet-based company. As you read, notice the boldfaced vocabulary. Try to guess the meaning from the context.

E-BUSINESS MAGAZINE
Profiles: Etsy.com

1   Do you see the same products in every store? Do you want **unique** items—things that are different and one-of-a-kind? My answer is "Yes!" And that is why I shop at Etsy.com®.

2   Etsy is an online **marketplace**—people can buy many unique things there. But Etsy is different. It is not just another Amazon.com® or eBay®.

3   First, I can find unique items from all over the world. Customers buy **crafts**, such as handmade jewelry and furniture. They also find other rare products, such as watches and old clothing. You can't find these items in stores, certainly not in big-box stores. I love that!

4   Second, when I shop at Etsy, I know I am helping the **vendors**, the individuals who sell things. Most of these vendors are the **artisans**, that is, the people who make their items by hand. They care about their crafts, their business, and their customers.

5   Lastly, the customer service is great. I get all of the benefits of shopping at a small business. I can ask the vendors questions online, and they quickly answer me. Also, my items arrive carefully wrapped[1] by the craftsperson, not by a machine.

---

[1] **wrapped:** covered with pretty paper

6 There is one small disadvantage. Because the items are unique or handmade, sometimes it is not possible to return them to the vendor. That is an advantage of a big-box store. (But I am happy with everything from Etsy.)

7 Online shopping is usually fast but not very personal. Etsy changes that. It is convenient and fast, but it is also personal. Etsy brings people together. This makes Etsy unique and exciting.

8 Visit Etsy.com and see for yourself.

COMPREHENSION

Complete the sentences with information from the reading.

1. Etsy is _____

2. The vendors are _____

3. Customers can _____

4. Shopping on Etsy is _____

■■□■□■■□■□■■□■□■■□■□■■□■□■■□■□■■■ *GO TO* MyEnglishLab *FOR MORE VOCABULARY PRACTICE.*

READING SKILL

1 Look at Reading Two again. Find the words in the text. Use the paragraph (¶) numbers to help you. Based on what you read, choose the correct definition of each word. Do not use a dictionary. Write the letter on the line. Then underline the words, phrases, and punctuation in the text that helped you understand the words.

Words	Definitions
_____ 1. unique (paragraph 1)	a. a space where people buy and sell things
_____ 2. marketplace (paragraph 2)	b. people who make things by hand
_____ 3. crafts (paragraph 3)	c. people who sell things
_____ 4. vendors (paragraph 4)	d. things made by hand using special talent or skill
_____ 5. artisans (paragraph 4)	e. special or different from other things

(continued on next page)

USING CONTEXT CLUES

Sometimes you can find the meaning of a word from the **context**, or the words, phrases, and sentences around the word. These helpful words, phrases, or sentences are called **context clues**.

Commas (, . . .,) or dashes (—. . .—) often suggest a context clue. Notice that *or the words, phrases, and sentences around the word* in the sentence above is a context clue. It helps you understand what *context* means.

That is, . . . can suggest an explanation, or context clue.

Such as . . . (followed by examples) can also suggest a context clue.

For example, the word *unique* in paragraph 1 means one-of-a-kind. The context clue is "—things that are different or one-of-a-kind." The dash (—) suggests the context clue.

Look at these other examples:

marketplace
context clue: "—people can buy many unique things there."

crafts
context clue: "**such as** hand-made jewelry and furniture."

vendors
context clue: "vendors, **the individuals who sell things**."

artisans
context clue: "**that is**, the people who make their items by hand."

2 Look at Reading One again. Find the words in the text. Use the paragraph (¶) numbers to help you. Based on what you read, choose the correct definition of each word and write the letter on the line. Do not use a dictionary. Then underline the words, phrases, and punctuation in the text that helped you understand the words.

Words	Definitions
_____ **1.** lose (paragraph 3)	**a.** useful or easy
_____ **2.** care (paragraph 5)	**b.** not to have something any more
_____ **3.** save (paragraph 7)	**c.** to think that something is important
_____ **4.** convenient (paragraph 8)	**d.** keep something so you can use it later

GO TO MyEnglishLab *FOR MORE SKILL PRACTICE.*

STEP 1: Organize

Check (✓) the benefits of each kind of business.

	MOM AND POP STORES	BIG-BOX CHAIN STORES	ETSY.COM
LOW PRICES			
MANY DIFFERENT PRODUCTS			
UNIQUE ITEMS			
HAND-MADE GOODS			
PERSONAL ATTENTION			
KNOWLEDGEABLE STAFF			
CONVENIENCE			
EASY COMMUNICATION			
OTHER: _____			

STEP 2: Synthesize

1 Imagine you are starting a business. What ideas from the readings are important to you? Fill in a short business plan describing your business or service.

1. What is the product or service? _____

2. How much is it? _____

3. Who are your customers? _____

4. Where will you sell this product or service?

_____ online

_____ in a small store

_____ in a chain store

2 In your notebook, write a short paragraph about your business. Use the information from the chart.

GO TO MyEnglishLab *TO CHECK WHAT YOU LEARNED.*

VOCABULARY

REVIEW

Complete the passage. Choose the correct word.

Hi. My name is Judy. I am an _____, and I sell my
1. (artisan / employee)

handmade jewelry—mostly earrings and necklaces—on Etsy. For many

years I made jewelry in my free time. Then my friends said, "Those are

beautiful! You should sell them." Now I do. I am the _____
2. (product / owner)

of a small business on Etsy. I opened my Etsy _____ in
3. (shop / customer)

September last year.

I enjoy being a _____ on Etsy. I have a full-time job during the day. I'm
4. (vendor / customer)

a waitress. At night and on weekends, I make jewelry and run my business. Etsy makes this

possible for me. I have no _____. I make everything by myself. I am very busy,
5. (employees / crafts)

but I love it.

Today my business is growing. I sell my products in an international _____,
6. (service / marketplace)

not just local. I have _____ in my neighborhood and around the world. I can
7. (prices / customers)

communicate with people around the world.

I care about my jewelry. I enjoy making and selling it to people. With Etsy, I can give my

customers _____—even if I can't meet them face-to-face.
8. (personal attention / marketplaces)

Are the holidays coming? Or your mother's birthday? Try _____ online at
9. (shopping / selling)

Etsy. You'll find thousands of _____ items for someone special. Be sure to visit
10. (free / unique)

Judy's Jewels while you are on Etsy.

GERUNDS

A *gerund* is a noun that ends in *-ing*.

Gerunds name activities, such as *shopping, speaking,* or *riding*. In a sentence, a gerund can be a **subject** or an **object**.

For example:

[subject]   [gerund subject]
Movies are fun.   **Going** to the movies is fun.

        [object]   [gerund object]
Sofia enjoys **movies**.   Sofia enjoys **going** to movies.

Verbs such as *enjoy* and *spend time* can have a gerund as an object.

NOTE: A **gerund phrase** is a gerund + the words that go with it.

Sofia enjoys **going to movies**.   **Riding a bicycle** is good exercise.

---

1 Match the beginning of the sentence with the end. Write the letter on the line.

	Subject	**Verb + Object**
_e_	**1.** Owning a business . . .	**a.** is interesting sometimes.
____	**2.** Shopping online . . .	**b.** but it is not the most important thing in life.
____	**3.** Saving money in the bank . . .	**c.** is important for your future.
____	**4.** Making money is important, . . .	**d.** is very convenient.
____	**5.** Communicating with people from other countries . . .	**e.** ~~is hard work for the owner.~~

	Subject + Verb	**Object**
____	**6.** Every morning I enjoy . . .	**f.** going to the dentist.
____	**7.** My hobby is . . .	**g.** collecting coins.
____	**8.** I don't like . . .	**h.** reading the newspaper online.
____	**9.** My little sister likes . . .	**i.** riding our bikes around the city.
____	**10.** We spend a lot of time . . .	**j.** playing with her toys.

2 Complete each sentence with a gerund or gerund phrase.

1. I enjoy _____.

2. _____ is one of my favorite things to do.

3. I don't enjoy _____.

4. _____ is really boring.

5. I spend a lot of time _____.

CREATE

Work with two or three partners. Write phrases and sentences to complete the journalist's interviews. Use words from the vocabulary sections on pages 76 and 86. Then present your dialogue to the class.

artisans	marketplace	personal attention	shop
crafts	own	prices	shopping
customer	owner	product	unique
employees	owning	service	vendors

WAYLON FLUFFINGS: Good morning. This is Waylon Fluffings for *The Morning Report*. I'm reporting from the outdoor market in

Prospect Park in Brooklyn, New York. Let's talk to one of the vendors here, Madeline Ortiz, from Salem Farms. Hello, Ms. Ortiz. You work for Salem Farms . . .

MADELINE ORTIZ: Well, actually I'm not just an employee. I'm the_____

WF: Oh, sorry. My mistake. What do you sell? And why do you think customers shop here?

MO: _____

_____

WF: Thanks very much for speaking with us, Ms. Ortiz. And now, let's talk to some shoppers. Here are Jeanne Lambert and Laszlo Arvai. Ms. Lambert, why do you come to this market?

JEANNE LAMBERT: Well, _____

_____

WF: And, Mr. Arvai, do you enjoy shopping here?

LAZLO ARVAI: Usually I don't like shopping, but I do enjoy _____ here. I just bought (a / some) _____ as a gift for my mother. It's _____

_____

WF: That's great. Thank you both very much. I'm Waylon Fluffings and it's a beautiful morning here in Brooklyn's Prospect Park, so come on down and check out this amazing marketplace.

GO TO MyEnglishLab *FOR MORE VOCABULARY PRACTICE.*

GRAMMAR

1 Read the email from Young-Hee to her friend from university, Sofia. Answer the questions. Then discuss your answers with a partner.

June 15th

Dear Sofia,

How are you? I miss you, and I miss school. But I am happy to be back in Seoul, too.

Seoul is a little different now. I am really upset about one change. There is a big Samsung-Mart coming to my beautiful neighborhood! I can't believe it!

My neighborhood is near Yonsei University in Seoul. It is very quiet here. There isn't a lot of noise. There are a lot of students and professors in my neighborhood. There are also many family-owned businesses on the main street. There is a flower shop. Also, there are two clothing stores, a bakery, a vegetable shop, and a pharmacy. There aren't any big-box chain stores—yet. I hope we don't lose these small stores when Samsung-Mart comes. I don't want my neighborhood to change any more. Oh, well.

I hope you are OK. Can you visit Korea soon? We can go to Samsung-Mart together. Just kidding!

Young-Hee

1. How many times does Young-Hee use *there is, there isn't, there are,* and *there aren't*? Underline them.

2. What nouns follow *there is* and *there isn't*? Make a list.

3. What nouns follow *there are* and *there aren't*? Make a list.

THERE IS / THERE ARE

1. Use **there is** or **there are** to state facts about something in the **present**.

   There is + singular count noun — **There is a bank** on Main Street.

   There are + plural count noun — **There are a lot of students** in my neighborhood.

   There is + non-count noun — **There is a lot of traffic** in Seoul.

2. Use **there was** or **there were** to state facts about something in the past.

   There was a flower shop on my street.

   There were a lot of people on my street.

3. Use the contractions **isn't / aren't** and **wasn't / weren't** with **there** in the **negative**.

   There isn't a McDonald's® nearby.

   There weren't any big-box chain stores.

4. For **questions**, put **there** after **is / are** and **was / were**.

   Is there a movie theater nearby?

   Use **any** with **yes / no** questions about **plural nouns** and **non-count nouns**.

   Were there any restaurants in your neighborhood?

   Is there any traffic in your neighborhood at night?

5. Do not confuse *there is* and *there are* with *there* when you refer to place. *There* means "in that location."

   Seoul is a beautiful city. There are some beautiful parks **there** (in Seoul).

2 Read Sofia's reply to Young-Hee. Then choose the correct verbs to complete her sentences.

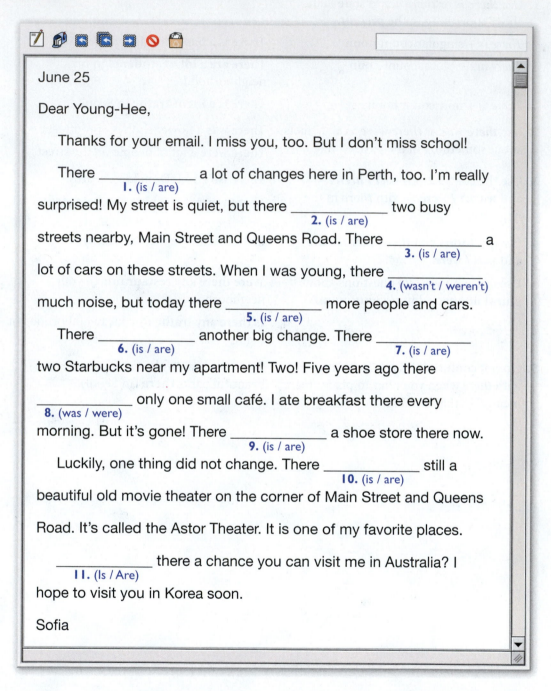

June 25

Dear Young-Hee,

Thanks for your email. I miss you, too. But I don't miss school!

There _____ a lot of changes here in Perth, too. I'm really
      I. (is / are)
surprised! My street is quiet, but there _____ two busy
                         2. (is / are)
streets nearby, Main Street and Queens Road. There _____ a
                                          3. (is / are)
lot of cars on these streets. When I was young, there _____
                                          4. (wasn't / weren't)
much noise, but today there _____ more people and cars.
                         5. (is / are)

There _____ another big change. There _____
      6. (is / are)   **7.** (is / are)
two Starbucks near my apartment! Two! Five years ago there

_____ only one small café. I ate breakfast there every
8. (was / were)
morning. But it's gone! There _____ a shoe store there now.
                                9. (is / are)

Luckily, one thing did not change. There _____ still a
                                   10. (is / are)
beautiful old movie theater on the corner of Main Street and Queens

Road. It's called the Astor Theater. It is one of my favorite places.

_____ there a chance you can visit me in Australia? I
II. (Is / Are)
hope to visit you in Korea soon.

Sofia

3 Work with a partner. Write five questions to ask about your partner's neighborhood or city. Use *Is / Are there* and *Was / Were there*. Then exchange books and answer each other's questions. Use *There is / are* and *There was / were*.

1. a. _____ Are there any fast-food restaurants nearby? _____

   b. _____ Yes, there are. There is a McDonald's. _____

2. a. _____

   b. _____

3. a. _____

   b. _____

4. a. _____

   b. _____

5. a. _____

   b. _____

6. a. _____

   b. _____

■■■■■■■■■■■■ **GO TO** MyEnglishLab *FOR MORE GRAMMAR PRACTICE AND TO CHECK WHAT YOU LEARNED.*

FINAL WRITING TASK

In this unit you read about locally-owned stores and large chain stores. You also read about the online marketplace, Etsy.

Now you are going to **write a paragraph describing a business that you recommend or a place you like to shop**. Use the vocabulary and grammar from the unit.*

---

* For Alternative Writing Topics, see page 99. These topics can be used in place of the writing topic for this unit or as homework. The alternative topics relate to the theme of the unit, but may not target the same grammar or rhetorical structures taught in the unit.

PREPARE TO WRITE: Brainstorming

1 Think about the different stores or businesses where you usually shop. Think only about brick-and-mortar stores (physical places), not online stores. Make a list in the chart under **Business**.

BUSINESS	LOCAL?	CHAIN?	BIG-BOX?	NOTES

2 Now complete the chart. Check the appropriate boxes: Local, Chain, or Big-Box. Under Notes, write notes about this store. Then tell a partner about the stores.

3 Choose one place that you think is most interesting. You will write about this one.

4 In your notebook, answer some of these questions:

1. Is it a big-box store or a locally-owned business?

2. How convenient is it to shop there?

3. Who are the customers?

4. Who are the owners? Who are the employees?

5. What product or service does this business sell?

6. If I go there, what will I see?

7. When is this business open? What are the hours?

8. Where is this business?

9. Why do you like it?

10. How is the service? How are the prices?

Note: You don't have to use all the information from your questions. Use the information that you think is most important when you write your paragraph.

WRITE: Describing a place

When you describe something, put the information in a clear order for the reader.

You can also use an idea or a feeling to organize your paragraph. For example, if your favorite store is a "happy" place, describe all the happy things there.

Example

I always enjoy shopping for food at Sunshine Market. The space feels happy. The walls are painted yellow and green—bright, happy colors. There is a lot of light from the big windows. If you can't find something, you can ask the employees. There aren't any unfriendly employees there. They are all very helpful and friendly. They smile a lot. I think they enjoy working there. The prices are also lower than other food stores. That really makes me happy. Visit Sunshine Market when you are in my neighborhood.

When you describe something, you can also use space order—telling where things are. You can write about what you see when you walk into the room. You can describe what your eyes see when you look from right to left or from left to right.

Example

I always enjoy shopping at Veronica's. The store has a lot of unique items in the window. When you walk in, you see a big table on the left. It has unique jewelry and other handmade things. On the right, there is a section called "Artisians' Marketplace." There is beautiful handmade clothing for men and women from all over the world. Shopping at Veronica's is interesting and fun. I highly recommend it.

Notice that the description of Veronica's includes a clear description of the space and the feeling that shopping there is "interesting and fun."

1 Read the paragraph. Then answer the questions in your notebook.

"That's Amore" is my favorite restaurant. My husband and I like to go there. It's small and romantic. There are only ten tables along the wall. They are not too close together, so customers can talk easily. The lights are not too bright but not too dark. There is a candle on every table. They give the room a warm feeling. The kitchen is always very busy, but it is clean. "Amore" is Italian for "love." It's easy to feel the love at "That's Amore." Go there with someone you love.

1. What "feeling(s)" does the writer want to communicate? How do you know?

2. Which sentence does not belong in this description? Why?

2 Imagine you are a sitting in a fast food chain restaurant, such as McDonald's® or Wendy's®. Answer the questions in your notebook. Then write a short descriptive paragraph about the restaurant. Be sure to use space order and to focus on a feeling.

1. What are some things that you see? Make a list of five things.

2. What is the feeling you get from being there?

_____

_____

_____

_____

_____

_____

3 Now write the first draft of your paragraph about a business or place where you like to shop. Don't worry about the grammar. Just try to make the ideas clear.

USING ADJECTIVES IN DESCRIPTIONS

An **adjective** is a word that modifies, or describes, a noun.

a **helpful** employee   **low** prices   a **beautiful** shop

When you describe something in writing, use adjectives that show how things look, feel, smell, taste, or sound.

Prepositional phrases can help to add details and show location. A prepositional phrase is a group of words that begins with a preposition (*in, on, at, between, from,* etc.)

> candles **on** every table
>
> tables **along** the wall
>
> a handsome man **in** a really nice suit
>
> **across** the top **of** the page
>
> **from** left **to** right

1 Read the paragraph. Underline the seven adjectives. The first one has been done for you.

> BuyBooks.com is a <u>terrible</u> website. I do not recommend it. First, it is very slow. Most websites are very fast—just click, click, click and you are finished. BuyBooks.com is different. I was on BuyBooks.com for 15 minutes to buy just a book. Second, it is a very confusing website. Next time, I will go to a better website or to a brick-and-mortar bookstore.

2 Complete the paragraph with the words or phrases from the box.

comfortable	huge	near my house
friendly	~~interesting~~	next to the window

> I recommend The Night Owl Bookshop. It is a great place to buy books. It is open late at night. It has a lot of _____*interesting*_____ books. For example, it has a _____
> (1)   (2)
> collection of comic books. I also like the feeling in The Night Owl Bookshop. There are a
>
> lot of _____ chairs. My favorite chair is _____. The
>   (3)   (4)
> employees are very _____. They always say hello. I'm glad that The Night
>   (5)
> Owl Bookshop is _____. I think you should go there.
>   (6)

Look at the first draft of your paragraph. Underline the descriptive adjectives and prepositional phrases you used. Add descriptive adjectives and prepositional phrases where you can.

GO TO MyEnglishLab FOR MORE SKILL PRACTICE.

EDIT: Writing the Final Draft

Go to MYENGLISHLAB and write the final draft of your paragraph. Check your grammar, spelling, capitalization, and punctuation. Check that you used some of the grammar and vocabulary from the unit. Use the checklist to help you write your final draft. Then give your paragraph to your teacher.

FINAL DRAFT CHECKLIST

❏ Did you describe a business?

❏ Did you begin with a good topic sentence?

❏ Did you use *there is / are* correctly?

❏ Did you use descriptive adjectives and prepositional phrases?

❏ Did you use vocabulary from the unit?

UNIT PROJECT

Work in a small group. Find an online store, describe it, and write an ad to sell a product or service on the website. Follow these steps:

STEP 1: Choose a website.

STEP 2: Write a paragraph describing the online store and what people can buy.

STEP 3: Choose one item on the website. Prepare an ad (in writing or video) to make people visit the website and want to buy the item. Look at the ad on page 77 as a model.

STEP 4: Present your ad to the class.

ALTERNATIVE WRITING TOPICS

Write about one of the topics. Use grammar and vocabulary from the unit.

1. Write a paragraph describing a place that is not a business. For example, write about your classroom or a room in your house.

2. In many places, large businesses are becoming more popular. Small, locally-owned businesses are going out of business. Is this a good change? Why or why not? Write your answer in one paragraph.

3. Do you enjoy shopping? If so, write a paragraph about why you like it. If not, write a paragraph about why you do not like it.

GO TO MyEnglishLab TO WRITE ABOUT ONE OF THE ALTERNATIVE TOPICS, WATCH A VIDEO ABOUT SELLING HOT DOGS, AND TAKE THE UNIT 4 ACHIEVEMENT TEST.

WHAT ARE YOU Afraid Of?

1 FOCUS ON THE TOPIC

1. What do you see in the photo?

2. How do you feel about the thing in the photo?

3. What are some things that people fear, perhaps for no reason?

GO TO MyEnglishLab TO CHECK WHAT YOU KNOW.

VOCABULARY

1 Read the list of words, definitions, and sentences.

afraid (of): scared of something that may hurt you. *I am afraid of spiders.*

fear (1): a feeling of great worry. *I have a fear of snakes.*

fear (2): be afraid of someone or something. *I fear snakes.*

panic: suddenly feel afraid and do things quickly without thinking. *People panic when someone cries, "Fire!"*

avoid: stay away from someone or something. *I avoid scary neighborhoods at night.*

embarrassed: feeling worried and unhappy about what other people think of you. *I feel embarrassed when everyone looks at me.*

relaxed: calm and not worried. *They feel very relaxed on the beach.*

normal: usual or expected. *It's normal to feel afraid sometimes. Everyone does.*

phobia: a strong fear of something. *I have a phobia of snakes.*

2 Use the words from the list to complete the poster.

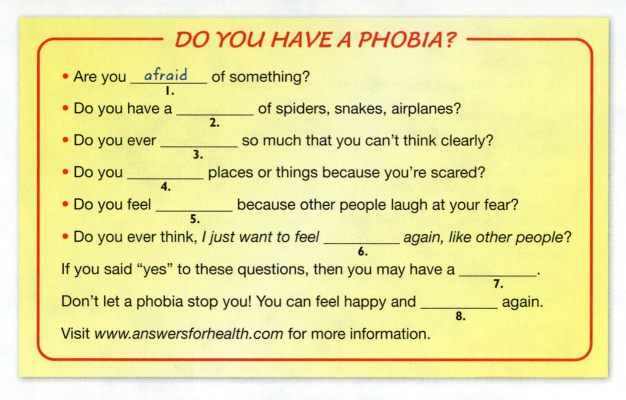

DO YOU HAVE A PHOBIA?

• Are you __afraid__ of something?
  1.

• Do you have a _____ of spiders, snakes, airplanes?
  2.

• Do you ever _____ so much that you can't think clearly?
  3.

• Do you _____ places or things because you're scared?
  4.

• Do you feel _____ because other people laugh at your fear?
  5.

• Do you ever think, *I just want to feel _____ again, like other people*?
  6.

If you said "yes" to these questions, then you may have a _____.
  7.

Don't let a phobia stop you! You can feel happy and _____ again.
  8.

Visit *www.answersforhealth.com* for more information.

GO TO MyEnglishLab *FOR MORE VOCABULARY PRACTICE.*

PREVIEW

You are going to read part of a website called *answersforhealth.com*. On this website, Dr. Hope Perry helps people when they are worried or sick. Dr. Perry got an email from Ann because Ann has a fear of spiders.

What will Dr. Perry say to Ann? Check (✓) the answers you think are correct.

_____ "Most spiders cannot hurt you."

_____ "Your fear is not normal."

_____ "Try to relax."

_____ "Read about spiders."

_____ Your ideas: _____

Now read the email.

Subject: Help! I'm Scared!

1   Dear Dr. Perry,

I have a problem, and I hope you can help me. Last month when I went up into the attic of my house, a big spider fell into my hair. I started to **panic**! I ran from the attic, down into the house, and out the door. My heart was racing,[1] and I felt sick.

2   Now, I am **afraid** all the time. In the morning I look for spiders in my shoes. At night I can't sleep because a spider may fall in my hair. I **avoid** going to the attic because of spiders. Also, I feel alone. I feel **embarrassed** because my family laughs at me. My family says, "Relax! Spiders are small!" But I never feel **relaxed**. I'm always worried.

3   Can you help? I need some advice.

Ann

4   Dear Ann,

I understand. Don't worry. A lot of people are afraid of spiders, so fearing spiders is **normal**. Spiders have many long legs, and people don't like that. Also, their webs look dirty. But most spiders are not dangerous, so they cannot hurt you.

5   But for some people, a normal fear becomes a **phobia**. When you have a phobia, you cannot have a normal life. You can't do normal things. Other people may laugh at you, but they don't understand your fear. Don't be embarrassed.

6   Why do we have phobias? Sometimes they start with a bad experience. Sometimes we learn a fear from our parents. Sometimes there is no reason.

7   You might have *arachnophobia*, the fear of spiders. When you see a spider, you might have a panic attack. A panic attack is when your heart beats very fast, or you may feel sick. It might also be difficult for you to think.

You can get help for *arachnophobia*. Here is some advice:

8   — Read about spiders, so you will be less afraid.
    — Look at photos of spiders, both live and dead ones. After some time, you will feel better.
    — Try to relax when you see a spider. Think about something nice.
    — Talk about your fear with family, friends, or a doctor.

9   Good luck to you, Ann!

Dr. Perry

---

[1]**racing:** moving very fast

MAIN IDEAS

1 Look again at your predictions in the Preview section on page 103. Circle your predictions that match the information in the reading.

2 Read each sentence. Circle the best answer.

1. Ann needs help because _____.

    a. her bedroom has spiders

    b. her fear is a big problem

2. It is <u>not</u> normal to _____.

    a. be afraid of spiders

    b. have a phobia of spiders

3. A phobia means you _____.

    a. can't do normal things because you are scared

    b. can't do normal things because you are embarrassed

4. Dr. Perry gives _____ to help people with phobias.

    a. medicine

    b. help

DETAILS

Read Ann's story again. Find the incorrect word in each sentence. Draw a line through the incorrect word, and write the correct word above it.

(1.) Ann's phobia started when a spider fell in her ~~shoe~~ *hair*. (2.) Now Ann can't eat, and she always feels afraid. (3.) Dr. Perry thinks Ann may have a spider. (4.) Phobias can come from a good experience, parents, or nothing. (5.) When Dr. Perry sees a spider, she may have a panic attack. (6.) That means her heart beats very fast, she feels relaxed, and she can't think. (7.) Dr. Perry tells Ann to read about spiders, look at pictures of spiders, relax, and laugh about the fear.

MAKE INFERENCES

INFERRING MEANING

An **inference** is an **"educated" guess** about something. The information is **not stated directly** in the reading. Sometimes writers give their ideas directly. For example, in paragraph 2, Ann writes, "Now, I feel afraid all the time." When we read Ann's words, we understand that she feels scared. Ann's meaning is clear.

Sometimes writers give their ideas indirectly. Good readers use what they read and what they already know to **infer what the writer means.**

  Read the question below and circle the best answer. Then read the explanation.

In paragraph 2, Ann writes, "my family laughs at me. My family says, 'Relax! Spiders are small!'"

What does Ann probably mean?

a. Her family thinks spiders are scary.
b. Her family doesn't think Ann is really afraid.
c. Her family is not afraid of spiders.

We already know that most people do not laugh when they are afraid. We also know that people are usually not relaxed when they are afraid. From what Ann writes, we can **infer** that she means her family is <u>not</u> afraid of spiders. The best answer is *c*.

Read each statement. Circle the correct answer.

1. In paragraph 4, Dr. Perry writes, "Don't worry." What does Dr. Perry probably mean?

   a. "Your fear is silly."

   b. "Being afraid is ok."

   c. "Spiders cannot hurt you."

2. In paragraph 5, Dr. Perry writes, "Don't be embarrassed." What does Dr. Perry probably mean?

   a. "Laughing is fun."

   b. "People will not laugh."

   c. "Your fear is not funny."

3. In paragraph 8, Dr. Perry writes, "Read about spiders, so you will be less afraid." What does Dr. Perry probably mean?

   a. "Books help you feel better."

   b. "You will understand spiders."

   c. "You can learn how to kill spiders."

EXPRESS OPINIONS

Arachnophobia is only one kind of phobia. Some people are afraid of other things. Look at the list below.

- snakes
- clowns
- going to the dentist
- small spaces
- very high places
- dogs or other animals

Work with a partner. For each item in the list, discuss your opinions about phobias by completing one of the sentences.

- People may be **afraid of** _____ because . . .

_____

- I know someone who is **afraid of** _____ because . . .

_____

■■■■■■■■■■■■■■■■■■■■■ *GO TO* MyEnglishLab *TO GIVE YOUR OPINION ABOUT ANOTHER QUESTION.*

READING TWO   OTHER PHOBIAS

READ

1 Look at the boldfaced words and phrases in the reading on page 108 and think about the questions.

1. Which of these words do you know?

2. What do the words mean?

2 Read about people with other phobias.

OTHER PHOBIAS

1   Elisa has *ophidiophobia*. *Ophidiophobia* is the fear of snakes. People think snakes are **disgusting** because snakes look dirty and wet. Snakes are not disgusting. They are clean and dry. Most people with a snake phobia have never seen or touched a real snake! These people are afraid, so they avoid parks and other places where snakes live.

a snake

2   Rosa has *acrophobia*. *Acrophobia* is the fear of high places. All people have some fear of high places. When people have *acrophobia*, they panic. As a result, they can't be in a tall building. They can't walk on a high bridge.

a tall building

3   Sam has *trypanophobia*. *Trypanophobia* is the fear of **needles**. This fear usually starts in childhood. When children visit the doctor, they cry because needles hurt. When children are older, they learn to relax. People with a phobia never relax. Because they cannot relax, they panic, or they avoid the doctor.

a needle

4   Ali has *glossophobia*. *Glossophobia* is the fear of public speaking. People with *glossophobia* speak easily with friends and people at work. They panic when a lot of people are watching and listening. They have wet hands because they **sweat** a lot.

a man afraid of public speaking

COMPREHENSION

Read the sentences. Write **T** (true) or **F** (false). When a sentence is false, cross out the incorrect information and write correct information.

_____ **1.** The fear of public speaking usually starts when a child goes to the doctor.

_____ **2.** When people have a fear of high places, they panic in tall buildings or on high bridges.

_____ **3.** People with a fear of snakes avoid going to the attic.

_____ **4.** People with a fear of public speaking panic when they talk to friends or people at work.

READING SKILL

1 Look at paragraph 1 of Reading Two again. The writer says some people think snakes are **disgusting**. Based on what you read, why do people think snakes are disgusting? Check (✓) the best answer. Then underline the words or phrases in the text that helped you answer the question.

_____ snakes live in parks and other places

_____ people have *ophidiophobia*

_____ snakes look dirty and wet

IDENTIFYING CAUSE AND EFFECT

When we understand how different ideas connect, we can understand a reading better.

Often, ideas are connected by **cause** and **effect**. The **cause** answers the question *Why did something happen?* The **effect** answers the question *What is the result?*

The word *because* tells you that the writer is stating the cause. *Because* can be at the beginning or end of the sentence.

[effect]   [cause]
People think snakes are disgusting **because** snakes look dirty and wet.

[cause]   [effect]
Because snakes look dirty and wet, people think snakes are disgusting.

The word *so* and the expression *as a result* show that the writer is talking about the effects.

[cause]   [effect]
Snakes look dirty and wet, **so** people think snakes are disgusting.

[cause]   [effect]
Snakes look dirty and wet. **As a result**, people think snakes are disgusting.

Look at the chart. Use ideas from Reading Two to complete the **Cause** and **Effect** columns. Underline the words in Reading Two that helped you understand.

PARAGRAPH	CAUSE	EFFECT
1	People with a snake phobia are afraid of snakes.	They avoid parks and other places where snakes live.
2	When people have acrophobia, they panic.	*They can't be in a tall building. They can't walk on a high bridge.*
3		Children cry.
4	People with trypanophobia never relax in a doctor's office.	

GO TO MyEnglishLab *FOR MORE SKILL PRACTICE.*

STEP 1: Organize

Look at Readings One and Two again. Use the information in the readings to complete Dr. Perry's chart.

	ANN	ELISA	ROSA	SAM	ALI
NAME OF PHOBIA					
THE FEAR OF					
EFFECT / RESULTS					

STEP 2: Synthesize

1 Imagine you are Dr. Perry. Continue the chart from Step 1. Write suggestions for each person.

	ANN	ELISA	ROSA	SAM	ALI
SUGGESTIONS	-Read about spiders -Look at photos of spiders -Try to relax when you see a spider -Talk about your fear of spiders	Read about snakes Look at photos of snakes		-Look at photos of needles	
			-Try to relax when you see a high place -Talk about your fear of high places	-Talk about your fear of needles	

2 Work with a partner. Student 1: You are **Elisa**, **Rosa**, **Sam**, or **Ali**. Talk about your fear. Student 2: You are **Dr. Perry**. Give suggestions to Student 1. Then switch roles. Take turns talking about a fear and giving suggestions. Use information from the charts in Step 1 and Step 2.

STUDENT 1: Dr. Perry, I have a phobia of _____. Because of my fear,

_____

STUDENT 2: I understand. I have some advice. _____

_____

STUDENT 1: Thanks for your help, Dr. Perry. I will try your ideas.

GO TO MyEnglishLab TO CHECK WHAT YOU LEARNED.

VOCABULARY

REVIEW

Complete the paragraphs by unscrambling the words in parentheses.

Experts say that anyone can have a (pahibo) _____. A

(nlmrao) _____ person like you or me can have a fear. Even

a famous person like Jackie Chan can have a fear.

Jackie Chan is a movie star from Hong Kong. In his movies, Jackie does

dangerous things. For example, he may fall from a tall building. In real life,

Jackie Chan is (arfdia) _____ of something. He has a fear of (nedesle)
3.

_____.
4.

Many people have this fear. These people (aswte) _____ when they
5.

see a needle. They (pnica) _____ at the doctor's office. They (viaod)
6.

_____ doctors. It is difficult for them to feel (raelxde) _____.
7. 8.

They think that needles are (ugdsgtsini) _____.
9.

If you think you have a phobia, talk about your (frae) _____ with friends or
10.

family. Don't feel (erambrssade) _____. You are not alone.
11.

ADJECTIVES + PREPOSITIONS

We can use some adjectives alone or with specific prepositions. These prepositions connect the adjectives to other words in the sentence.

Examples

I saw the spider, and I was **afraid.**

I am **afraid of** spiders.

 NOT: *I am afraid about spiders.*

I felt **embarrassed** when my family laughed.

I am **embarrassed about** my phobia.

 NOT: *I am embarrassed of my phobia.*

Study the list of adjective + preposition combinations.

afraid **of**	happy **about**	nervous **about**	scared **of**
embarrassed **about**	interested **in**	relaxed **about**	

Read the sentences. Circle the correct preposition.

1. Jackie Chan is afraid (*of* / *about*) needles.

2. I'm happy (*of* / *about*) your advice.

3. I am interested (*about* / *in*) phobias.

4. Ann never feels relaxed (*of* / *about*) spiders.

5. A person with acrophobia feels nervous (*of* / *about*) high places.

6. Ali is scared (*of* / *in*) public speaking.

7. You shouldn't be embarrassed (*about* / *of*) your fear.

8. Some people are afraid (*of* / *in*) dogs.

CREATE

Write five sentences that are true for you. Use five adjectives from the box and the correct prepositions.

| afraid | embarrassed | happy | interested | nervous | relaxed | scared |

Example

I am interested in reading books.

1. _____
2. _____
3. _____
4. _____
5. _____

GO TO MyEnglishLab *FOR MORE VOCABULARY PRACTICE.*

GRAMMAR

1 Max is a person who has a problem. On *answersforhealth.com*, Dr. Perry chats with people who need help. Read part of their online conversation. Pay attention to the boldfaced words. Underline the verbs. Then study the charts below.

MAX: **Can** you help me? My friend asked me to visit his house. But I **can't** go to my friend's house. I'm scared.

DR. PERRY: Why are you scared?

MAX: I'm afraid of cats. I **can't** go to my friend's house because he has a cat. The cat **may** hurt me.

DR. PERRY: I **can** help you. Tell me, is the cat mean? Did it hurt you in the past?

MAX: No, the cat isn't mean. But I'm afraid.

DR. PERRY: You **might** have a phobia. First, call your friend. Tell him about your fear. He **will** understand.

MAX: OK, but I still feel scared.

DR. PERRY: Read about cats. You **may** feel less scared.

2 Look again at the boldfaced words in Exercise 1. What form of verb comes after each boldfaced word?

MODALS: *CAN, MAY, MIGHT,* AND *WILL*	
1. *Can, may, might,* and *will* are **modals.** Always use the **base form of the verb** after modals.	[base form] I **can help** you. [base form] The cat **may hurt** me. [base form] You **might have** a phobia. [base form] He **will understand.**
2. The negative of modals is **modal** + *not.* Always use **the base form of the verb** after **modal** + *not.*	[base form] The cat **cannot hurt** you. [base form] The cat **may not hurt** you. [base form] The cat **might not hurt** you. [base form] The cat **will not hurt** you.
3. Use *cannot* for *can* + *not.*	[base form] He **cannot understand** my fear.
4. Use *won't* for *will* + *not* in speaking and informal writing.	[base form] The cat **won't hurt** you.
5. Use *can't* in speaking and informal writing.	[base form] I **can't go** to my friend's house because he has a cat.
6. A modal changes the meaning of the verb that follows. *Can* often means **ability.** *May* and *might* often mean **possibility.** *Will* means a **future prediction.**	I **can** help you. I **can't** go to my friend's house. You **may** feel less scared. You **might** have a phobia. He **will** understand.

3 Read Dr. Perry's online chat with Kate. Complete each sentence with the correct modal and the verb in parentheses.

1. Use *can / can't.*

> **KATE:** Dr. Perry, I need help. I'm afraid of public speaking. But in my English
>
> class next week I need to do a presentation.
>
> I _____ in front of the other students. I
>   (speak)
>
> _____ of the correct words, and
>   (think)
>
> I _____ at the class. I'm scared!
>   (look)
>
> **DR. PERRY:** I _____ you. Don't worry, Kate. You
>   (help)
>
> _____ a good presentation.
>   (give)

2. Use *may / might* or *may not / might not.*

> **KATE:** Really?
>
> **DR. PERRY:** Yes. Many people have a fear of public speaking. Other students in your
>
> class _____ afraid, too.
>   (feel)
>
> **KATE:** I didn't think of that. You _____ right. That's good news!
>   (be)
>
> **DR. PERRY:** Of course! Public speaking is hard, so the presentation
>
> _____ easy. But that is normal.
>   (be)

3. Use *will / will not / won't.*

> **KATE:** OK. But everyone _____ at me when I speak.
>   (look)
>
> **DR. PERRY:** They are your friends. They _____ at you. They want you to
>   (laugh)
>
> feel relaxed, so they _____ politely.
>   (listen)
>
> **KATE:** I hope so. I _____ about your advice!
>   (think)

4 Phillip and his wife are going to Jamaica for vacation. Phillip is afraid of flying in airplanes. Choose the answers that complete Phillip's sentences.

1. On our vacation, flying in an airplane _____ be scary.
(will / can)

2. I _____ panic in the airplane.
(can / may)

3. Other people _____ laugh at me.
(might / can)

4. Sometimes when I'm afraid, I _____ think clearly.
(won't / can't)

5. My wife is not scared. She _____ fly with no problem.
(can / might)

5 Write five suggestions for Phillip, affirmative or negative. Use four different modals. Then share your sentences with the class.

1. _____

2. _____

3. _____

4. _____

5. _____

6 There are six mistakes in the sentences. The first mistake is already corrected. Find and correct five more mistakes.

1. A doctor can ~~to~~ help you.

2. Isabelle has a phobia of needles, so she no can go to the doctor.

3. Lisa may has a phobia of spiders.

4. She no will go in the attic, and she can't sleeping.

5. I might be have a phobia.

■■■■■■■■■■■ **GO TO** MyEnglishLab **FOR MORE GRAMMAR PRACTICE AND TO CHECK WHAT YOU LEARNED.**

FINAL WRITING TASK

In this unit, you read about people who have phobias. Some people have phobias, but all people feel afraid of something.

You are going to **write a response giving suggestions** to someone who is afraid. Use the vocabulary and grammar from the unit.*

Read the blog post from someone who wants help.

Advice Bloggers

Home   **About Us**   **Contact**

Moving to London

Posted by Brian

Date: November 24, 2013

I went to a job interview in London last week. I got the job! The company seems very good, and the work will be fun. Also, the people at the company are very nice. But the job is in London. That's so far away! I have always lived here in Charlotte, NC. My friends and family are here. I don't know anyone in London. I'm afraid of leaving my home and living in a new city. I need advice. Can you help?

-*Brian*, Charlotte, NC, USA

Leave a Comment

PREPARE TO WRITE: Brainstorming

To help you plan your response, you are going to brainstorm a list of suggestions for Brian.

1 Work with a partner. How can Brian feel better? What can he do? Make a list of ideas in the chart under **Suggestions**.

SUGGESTIONS	BRIAN WILL FEEL BETTER BECAUSE . . .
• Brian can chat with his family online.	• He won't feel alone.
•	•
•	•
•	•

2 Look again at your list. Say more about each idea. You might ask yourself, "Why will this help Brian?" or "How will this idea make Brian feel better?" Write your answers in the chart under **Brian will feel better because . . .**

---

* For Alternative Writing Topics, see page 123. These topics can be used in place of the writing topic for this unit or as homework. The alternative topics relate to the theme of the unit, but may not target the same grammar or rhetorical structures taught in the unit.

118   UNIT 5

3 Choose 2 or 3 ideas that are best or most interesting. You can use these ideas in your message to Brian.

WRITE: Making a Suggestion

When you make a suggestion follow these steps:

<u>**Steps for Making a Suggestion**</u>

1. Show that you understand the problem.

2. Give your suggestion.

3. Give a reason for your suggestion.

4. Conclude by offering help or a final comment.

1 Donna lives in Perth, Australia. Read Donna's message to an online group.

Advice Bloggers

Home   **About Us**   **Contact**

I work for a great company. I give personal attention to customers. I like speaking to one customer at a time, and customers like me. Last week, my boss offered me a better job at the company. I will make more money, and I will teach employees about giving personal attention. But I will have to speak to large groups of employees. I'm afraid of public speaking! I always panic and sweat. What can I do?

-Donna, Perth, Australia

Leave a Comment

---

2 Read the sentences. Think about the Steps for Making a Suggestion above. Put the sentences in order. Then compare your answers with a partner's.

_____ When you practice at home, you will get better at public speaking.

__1__ I was afraid of talking to groups too, so I think I understand your situation.

(continued on next page)

_____ A class might help you relax in front of a group.

__2__ You can take a class for public speaking.

_____ Also, you can practice at home every day.

_____ I'm sure you'll be great at your new job. Good luck!

3 Use the sentences in Exercise 2 to write a message to Donna. Then compare your message with a partner's.

Dear Donna,

_____

_____

_____

_____

_____

_____

_____

4 Now write the first draft of your message to Brian. Use the Steps for Making a Suggestion to help you.

REVISE

ADDING SUPPORTING DETAILS

Supporting details help to explain your ideas and make your writing more interesting. When you write, think about these questions:

- *Why is this idea important?*
- *How can I help my reader understand more easily what I mean?*
- *What examples can I give to make my idea clearer?*
- *What else can I write to make this more interesting?*

   Asking these questions can help you add supporting details to your writing.

1 Read the messages. The suggestions are underlined once. The supporting details are underlined twice.

Q: My friend is having a big party with a lot of people. I don't like parties! Being around a lot of people makes me nervous. I'm scared of talking to new people. I don't know what to talk about. Sometimes I panic. What can I do?

-Mary, Dublin, Ireland

A: I think I understand your problem. Talking with new people scares me, too. Just try to be
How?
friendly at the party. Smile and say hello. You can also write a list of ideas to talk about.
What?   *Why?*
Think about your list at the party. It will help you have something to talk about.
What?   *What?*
I always do this and it helps. I know what to talk about, so I feel more relaxed. You might

want to tell your friend how you feel before the party. And remember, there may be others
Why?
who are afraid, too. Sometimes you can be more relaxed because someone else knows

how you feel. You might even have some fun. It *is* a party! Good luck!

2 Write supporting details to complete the message. Then share your message with a partner.

A: I can understand how you feel. I feel nervous with new people too. You can go to the

party with a person you know. _____

_____

_____

Also, you might go home after one or two hours. _____

_____

_____

Good luck at the party!

3 Now look at the first draft of your message to Brian. What supporting details can you add? Make changes as needed.

GO TO MyEnglishLab *FOR MORE SKILL PRACTICE.*

EDIT: Writing the Final Draft

Go to MYENGLISHLAB and write the final draft of your message. Check your grammar, spelling, capitalization, and punctuation. Check that you used some of the grammar and vocabulary from the unit. Use the checklist to help you write your final draft. Then give your paragraph to your teacher.

FINAL DRAFT CHECKLIST

❏ Did you give suggestions to Brian?

❏ Did you begin with a good topic sentence?

❏ Did you use supporting details?

❏ Did you use basic modals (*can*, *will*, *may*, and *might*)?

❏ Did you use vocabulary from the unit?

UNIT PROJECT

Learn more about a phobia. Follows these steps:

STEP 1: Choose a phobia that you didn't read about in this unit. Some examples are the fear of dogs, the fear of clowns, the fear of dentists, or the fear of going to the doctor.

STEP 2: Look for information about the phobia. Read websites or talk to a person who has the phobia. Answer these questions:

- What is the name of the phobia?
- When a person has this phobia . . .
  - what does he/she fear?
  - how does he/she feel?
  - what problems does he/she have?
  - what places or things does he/she avoid?
- What suggestions can help people with this phobia?

STEP 3: Complete the chart with your information from Step 2.

PHOBIA	
FEAR OF	
RESULTS	
SUGGESTIONS	
OTHER INFORMATION	

STEP 4: Talk to a partner about his or her chart. Ask each other questions from Step 2. As you talk, add information to your chart.

STEP 5: Write a paragraph about this phobia. Share your paragraph with the class.

ALTERNATIVE WRITING TOPICS

Write about one of the topics. Use the vocabulary and grammar from the unit.

1. Not everyone has a phobia, but everyone has a fear. Write a paragraph about something you are afraid of. When did your fear start? Why? What can you do to feel better?

2. Some people like to be scared. Write a paragraph about a scary movie or a scary experience that you enjoyed.

GO TO MyEnglishLab *TO WRITE ABOUT ONE OF THE ALTERNATIVE TOPICS, WATCH A VIDEO ABOUT WEIRD PHOBIAS, AND TAKE THE UNIT 5 ACHIEVEMENT TEST.*

WHAT AN
Adventure!

1 FOCUS ON THE TOPIC

1. What is the *Spirit of St. Louis*?

2. Do you know the man in the picture? If yes, who is he? If not, what do you think he did?

3. Do you want to take a long trip in this airplane? Why or why not?

GO TO MyEnglishLab TO CHECK WHAT YOU KNOW.

VOCABULARY

Read the list of words and their definitions.

adventure: an exciting thing that someone does or that happens to someone

contest: a game that people try to win; a competition

flight: a trip in an airplane

hero: someone you respect very much for doing something good

landed: arrived somewhere in an airplane (past form of *land*)

media: (plural) newspapers, magazines, radio, and television

pilot: the person who flies an airplane

set a record: did something faster or better than ever before (past form of *set a record*)

took off: left a place in an airplane (past form of *take off*)

unforgettable: not possible to forget

Now read about Lindbergh's trip on the *Spirit of St. Louis*. **Complete the sentences with words from the list.**

In 1919, Raymond Orteig started a _____ *contest* _____. He offered $25,000 to the first
                                            1.

pilot to fly non-stop across the Atlantic Ocean between New York and Paris. In 1927, Charles

Lindbergh was the winner of the contest.

In the 1920s flying airplanes was a new science. Charles Lindbergh, a young airmail

_____, was very interested in flying. When he found out about Orteig's
        2.

contest, he decided to enter it. He was ready for this great _____.
                                                                    3.

On May 10, 1927, Lindbergh _____ from San Diego, California. He
                                      4.

stopped in St. Louis, Missouri, for gas and oil. Then he quickly continued on to New York.

He _____ in New York on May 12th. His trip from San Diego to New York
        5.

was less than 22 hours. He _____ for the fastest _____ across
                                  6.   7.

the United States.

This was only the beginning of Lindbergh's historic trip. Lindbergh was on his way to

becoming an international _____. People from the _____,

8.   9.
—newspapers, magazines, and radio, followed him from that day until the end of his life. For

Lindbergh and people around the world, this was a(n) _____ experience.

10.

GO TO MyEnglishLab **FOR MORE VOCABULARY PRACTICE.**

PREVIEW

A *fool* is a person who is crazy or not very intelligent. At first, people called Lindbergh "The Flying Fool." Why do you think they called him this? Check (✓) the answers you think are correct.

_____ The weather was bad.

_____ Lindbergh was too young to fly.

_____ The plane was too small to cross the ocean.

_____ Lindbergh was not a good student in school.

_____ The trip was too long.

_____ Your ideas: _____

Now read the newspaper story about Lindbergh's historic trip from New York to Paris.

Lindbergh Did It!

By Jacques Moreau
Paris Express News **Staff Writer**

Paris Express News—May 27, 1927

1　PARIS, FRANCE—One week ago, Charles Lindbergh was just a handsome, 25-year-old airmail **pilot** from a small town in the United States. Today he is the most famous man in the world and the most important man in the history of flying.

2　Last week, Lindbergh started out on an **adventure**. He flew solo from New York to France. He was the first person to fly non-stop across the Atlantic Ocean alone. He also **set the record** for the longest non-stop **flight**.

3　Lindbergh **took off** on his historic flight on May 20th at 7:52 A.M. People called him "The Flying Fool." On that day, other pilots in the **contest** waited in New York because the weather was very bad. Lindbergh decided not to wait. He took five sandwiches, a bottle of water, a notebook, a pen, and a compass. He didn't even have a radio. All he heard was the sound of the wind and the noise from the plane's engine. He was in the air all alone with his thoughts, his hopes, and his fears.

4　After 3,610 miles, 33 hours and 30 minutes and no sleep, Lindbergh **landed** in Paris on May 21st. At that moment, his life changed forever. There were 150,000 excited people waiting to greet him. The international **media** were also there. Photographers and newspaper reporters wanted to be the first to tell Lindbergh's story. When he got out of his plane and saw all the excitement, he knew that his life would never be the same again.

5　When he began this **unforgettable** flight, he was a quiet young man from a quiet town. This morning, "Lucky Lindy" left Paris as an international **hero**.

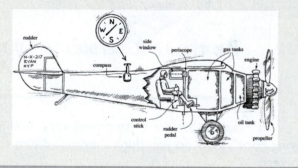

MAIN IDEAS

1　Look again at your predictions in the Preview section on page 127. Check your predictions that match the information in the reading.

2　Circle the best answer to complete each statement.

　1. In 1927, Lindbergh set the record for the _____ non-stop flight.

　　a. first

　　b. longest

　　c. highest

2. He was the first person to fly non-stop from _____.

    a. France to the United States

    b. The United States to France

    c. New York to San Diego

3. The people waiting in Paris were very _____.

    a. excited

    b. quiet

    c. confused

4. Because of his historic flight, Lindbergh became very _____.

    a. handsome

    b. lucky

    c. famous

DETAILS

Use one of the numbers from the box to answer each question. Write your answers in complete sentences.

150,000	3,610	7:52	one	the 21st
25	33½	five	the 20th	

1. How old was Lindbergh when he flew across the Atlantic?

_____*Lindbergh was 25 years old when he flew across the Atlantic*_____.

2. On what date did he take off from New York?

_____

3. At what time in the morning did he take off from New York?

_____

4. How many people were on Lindbergh's plane when he flew across the Atlantic?

_____

(continued on next page)

5. How many miles was Lindbergh's flight?

_____

6. For how many hours was he in the air?

_____

7. How many sandwiches did he take on his trip?

_____

8. On what date did he land in Paris?

_____

9. About how many people greeted him when he arrived in Paris?

_____

MAKE INFERENCES

MAKING INFERENCES ABOUT PEOPLE

An **inference** is **an "educated" guess** about something. The information is **not stated directly** in the reading. Good readers put ideas together to find the right answer. You can use what you already know and what you read in the text to **understand** more **about** a **person** in the reading.

We can understand what kind of person Charles Lindbergh was by thinking about his actions and his words. We also learn about Lindbergh from what other people (here, the writer) said about him.

For example:
Was Charles Lindbergh an adventurous person (liking excitement or adventures)?

From paragraph 3, we know that Lindbergh entered Orteig's contest, and he flew across the Atlantic in bad weather. He took off when other pilots stayed on the ground. He also flew alone. From this information, we can infer that Charles Lindbergh was adventurous.

Look at the reading again and at the list of adjectives. Do you think they describe Charles Lindbergh? Work with a partner. Ask and answer the question. Explain your answer by pointing to ideas in the reading.

Was he _____?

- determined (having a strong desire to do something)
- independent (liking to be alone, not needing other people)
- simple (not complicated)

- social (like talking with people)
- competitive (wanting to be the best at something)

Yes, he was. I think he was _____.

    In paragraph # _____ it says _____.

No, he wasn't. I don't think he was _____.

    In paragraph # _____ it says _____.

EXPRESS OPINIONS

Do you think Lindbergh was nervous before or after his flight? Explain your answers to a partner.

1. I think (don't think) he was nervous before his flight because _____.

2. I think (don't think) he was nervous after his flight because _____.

■■■■■■■■■■■■■■■■■■■■ *GO TO* MyEnglishLab *TO GIVE YOUR OPINION ABOUT ANOTHER QUESTION.*

READING TWO   CRASH LANDING ON THE HUDSON RIVER

READ

1 Look at the boldfaced words in the reading on page 132 and think about the questions.

1. Which of these words do you know?

2. What do the words mean?

Crash Landing on the Hudson River

New York Daily Post
By Sally Martinez
Staff Writer

1   On January 15, 2009, U.S. Airways flight 1549 took off from LaGuardia Airport in New York City. It was going to Charlotte, North Carolina. There were 150 passengers and five crew members on board—the pilot, the co-pilot, and three flight attendants. The flight seemed like any trip, but very quickly it became an unforgettable adventure.

2   Unfortunately, three minutes after take off, a flock of birds hit the plane's engines. First, the left engine was on fire and stopped working. Then, the second engine also stopped.

3   Captain Chesley "Sully" Sullenberger, the pilot, had to make a fast decision. He did not have enough time to fly back to LaGuardia. He had to do something. If he did nothing, then everyone on the plane was going to die, including himself. Sullenberger decided to land on the Hudson River. It was very **risky**, but he had to try. He used his experience as a pilot and as a glider[1] pilot to land the airplane on the Hudson River. As a result, all of the people on board the plane lived.

4   Days later, people called this **event** the "Miracle[2] on the Hudson." They couldn't believe it was possible to land such a big plane on a river. Passengers on the plane were very thankful to Sullenberger. One passenger told reporters, "Captain Sullenberger is the best pilot in the world." Another said, "He is a great leader! He should be the President of the United States."

5   Government officials will study this unforgettable event. They do not want it to happen again. For now, people are just happy to be alive. Everyone agrees: It was an adventure they do not want to repeat.

---

[1] **glider:** a very light plane with no engine

[2] **miracle:** something that happens that you thought was impossible; in religions, something only God can make happen

COMPREHENSION

Complete the sentences with information from the reading.

1. U.S. Airways Flight 1549 _____

2. A flock of birds _____

3. Captain Chesley Sullenberger _____

4. The passengers and crew _____

■ ■ *GO TO* MyEnglishLab *FOR MORE VOCABULARY PRACTICE.*

READING SKILL

Look at paragraph 4 of Reading Two again. Notice the information in bold. Which sentence is a fact (we know it's true)? Which is an opinion (people can agree or disagree)? Complete the chart.

Days later, people called this event the "Miracle on the Hudson." They couldn't believe it was possible to land such a big plane on a river. Passengers on the plane were very thankful to Sullenberger. One passenger told reporters, "**Captain Sullenberger is the best pilot in the world.**" Another said, "He is a great leader! He should be the President of the United States."

FACT	OPINION

(continued on next page)

UNDERSTANDING FACTS VS. OPINIONS

When you read, it is important to notice the difference between facts and opinions. A **fact** is something that we know is true. We can check the information and agree. An **opinion** is a personal idea or belief. People can agree with our opinions or disagree with them.

For example:

People called this event the "Miracle on the Hudson."

It is a fact that people called it a miracle. We can check the news reports. People really did call it the "Miracle on the Hudson."

Captain Sullenberger is the best pilot in the world.

This is an opinion. Captain Sullenberger is a very good pilot, but not everyone will agree that he is the best pilot in the world.

Look again at Reading One on page 128. Read each sentence. Decide if the sentence is a fact or an opinion. Write **F** (fact) or **O** (opinion).

_____ **1.** Charles Lindbergh was internationally famous.

_____ **2.** He set the record for the longest non-stop flight.

_____ **3.** Lindbergh was a fool.

_____ **4.** Lindbergh didn't take enough food on his flight.

_____ **5.** On the day that Lindbergh's plan took off, the weather was bad.

_____ **6.** He was very brave to fly solo across the Atlantic.

GO TO MyEnglishLab *FOR MORE SKILL PRACTICE.*

CONNECT THE READINGS

STEP 1: Organize

Look at Readings One and Two again. What did each man do? What happened after as a result? Complete the chart. Then discuss your answers with the class.

	CHARLES LINDBERGH	CHESLEY SULLENBERGER
WHAT DID HE DO?		
WHAT HAPPENED AS A RESULT?		

STEP 2: Synthesize

Some people call Charles Lindbergh and "Sully" Sullenberger heroes. Do you agree? Give your opinion based on the information in the chart in Step 1. Complete the first sentence. Then write two or three more sentences about each person.

1. I think Lindbergh (is / isn't) a hero because _____

_____

_____

2. I think Sullenberger (is / isn't) a hero because _____

_____

_____

■■■■■■■■■■■■■■■■■■■■■■■■■■■■■■■■■■■■ **GO TO** MyEnglishLab **TO CHECK WHAT YOU LEARNED.**

3 FOCUS ON WRITING

VOCABULARY

REVIEW

Read the story about Amelia Earhart. Choose the words that complete the sentences.

Amelia Earhart (1897–1937) was a ____*pilot*____. She
                             1. (pilot / writer)

became interested in flying while working in Canada during

World War I. She started flying in 1922.

In 1928, Earhart _____ across the Atlantic Ocean. She
                2. (flew / fly)

was the first woman to do this, but on this flight Earhart was not

the pilot. She was only a passenger.

This _____ made her very famous. She was a
        3. (flight / contest)

_____ to many women and girls. People called her "Lady Lindy."
4. (pilot / hero)

Then, in 1932, she _____ another record. She became the first woman to fly
           5. (set / flew)

solo across the Atlantic. She _____ from Harbour Grace, Newfoundland, and
            6. (took off / landed)

(continued on next page)

What an Adventure!   **135**

_____ near Londonderry, Ireland. In 1935, she became the first person to _____

7. (took off / landed)   8. (flew / fly)

solo from Hawaii to California.

In 1937, Earhart and another pilot, Fred Noonan, decided to fly around the world.

This flight was _____, but the danger did not stop Earhart. She wanted more

9. (lucky / risky)

_____.

10. (adventures / events)

Sadly, their plane was lost in the Pacific Ocean. No one knows exactly what happened

to them. It's a mystery. Even today there are stories in the _____ about Amelia

11. (media / adventures)

Earhart and her mysterious last flight.

Today people still read about Earhart's life. For them, her story is _____.

12. (lucky / unforgettable)

EXPAND

USING SYNONYMS

A *synonym* is a word that has a similar meaning to another word. Use synonyms to make your
writing more interesting.

The **price** of the *Spirit of St. Louis* was $10,580.
The **cost** of the *Spirit of St. Louis* was $10,580.

The plane was **built** in San Diego, California.
The plane was **constructed** in San Diego, California.

Read each sentence. Change the underlined word to a synonym from Reading One on page
128 and Reading Two on page 132. Follow the example.

took off

1. Lindbergh <u>departed</u> from New York on May 20, 1927.

2. The *Spirit of St. Louis* <u>arrived</u> in France on May 21, 1927.

3. He flew across the Atlantic <u>alone</u>.

4. Lindbergh won the <u>competition</u> that Orteig started in 1919.

5. The <u>press</u> gave Lindbergh a lot of attention in the newspapers and on the radio.

6. Lindbergh became <u>well known</u> all over the world.

7. His historic <u>trip</u> changed his life.

8. Amelia Earhart was another famous <u>flier</u>.

9. Sullenberger had to make a very fast <u>choice</u>.

10. Trying to land an airplane on a river was very <u>dangerous</u>.

CREATE

Imagine that you were a passenger on Flight 1549. Write a paragraph in your diary about that unforgettable event. What happened? How did you feel? Write at least five sentences.

Friday, January 16th

    Yesterday was a day that I will never forget. I really can't believe what

happened. First, _____

_____

_____

_____

_____

GO TO MyEnglishLab FOR MORE VOCABULARY PRACTICE.

GRAMMAR

1 Read the paragraph. Notice the boldfaced simple past verbs. Then answer the questions on the next page.

On March 1, 1932, someone **kidnapped** Charles and Anne Lindbergh's baby. The kidnapper **left** a note in the baby's bedroom. In the note, the kidnapper **asked** for $50,000. Lindbergh **paid** the money. Unfortunately, on May 12, 1932, someone **found** the baby. He **was** dead. In 1935, the police **arrested** Bruno Richard Hauptmann. Hauptmann **said**, "I **didn't do** it!" Many people **did not believe** him. The court **decided** that he **did** it. As a result, Hauptmann **died** in the electric chair[1] on April 2, 1936. Today, some people believe that Hauptmann **did not kidnap** the Lindbergh baby.

(continued on next page)

---

[1] **electric chair:** a chair that uses electricity to kill people as a punishment for a crime

1. Which past tense verbs are <u>regular</u>? Make a list.

2. Which past tense verbs are <u>irregular</u>? Make a list.

3. How do you form the simple past in negative sentences for regular verbs?

THE SIMPLE PAST

1. Use the **simple past** to talk about actions completed in the past.	People *called* Lindbergh "The Flying Fool."

	Base Form	Simple Past
2. To form the simple past:		
For **regular verbs**, add *-ed* to the **base form**.	land	land**ed**
	return	return**ed**
If the base form ends in *-e*, add only *-d*.	receive	receiv**ed**
	live	liv**ed**
	die	di**ed**
If the base form ends in a consonant followed by *-y*, change the *-y* to *-i* and add *-ed*.	marry	marr**ied**
	try	tr**ied**
If the base form ends with consonant-vowel-consonant, double the last consonant, then add *-ed*.	kidnap	kidnap**ped**
	stop	stop**ped**

	Base Form	Simple Past
3. Many verbs have irregular past forms.	become	**became**
	buy	**bought**
NOTE: The simple past of *be* is *was* or *were*, and the simple past of *have* is *had*.	do	**did**
	fly	**flew**
	go	**went**
	make	**made**
	take	**took**
	think	**thought**

4. To make **negative statements**, use: *didn't* (*did not*) + **the base form**	Lindbergh *didn't have* a radio with him.

5. To ask *wh-* questions, use: *Wh-* word + *did* + subject + **base form**	When *did* Earhart *disappear*?
	[subject]
NOTE: If you do not know the subject of the question, do not use *did*.	*Who kidnapped* the Lindberghs' baby? *What happened* to the Lindberghs' baby?

6. To ask *yes / no* questions, use: *Did* + subject + **base form**	*Did* Lindbergh *win* Orteig's contest?

2 Complete the paragraphs with the simple past form of the verbs.

Raymond Orteig _____*started*_____ the flying contest for two reasons. First, Orteig
1. (start)

_____ to build friendship between the United States and France. He also
2. (want)

_____ it _____ important for people to have an interest in flying.
3. (think)   4. (be)

Five pilots _____ to cross the Atlantic during the 1920s, but they
5. (try)

_____ successful. The flight _____ very risky. Six men
6. (not / be)   7. (be)

_____ trying to win the contest. Finally, Lindbergh _____ it. After
8. (die)   9. (do)

Lindbergh _____ in Paris, people _____ him a hero. Later, he
10. (arrive)   11. (call)

_____ one of the most famous men in the world.
12. (become)

Lindbergh _____ very independent. He _____ strong
13. (be)   14. (have)

opinions. For example, he _____ the United States to enter World War II.
15. (not / want)

He _____ that Germany _____ too strong. Many people
16. (believe)   17. (be)

_____ with his opinions. At that time, they _____ Lindbergh
18. (not / agree)   19. (not / think)

_____ a hero at all.
20. (be)

3 Write questions about Charles Lindbergh. Write three *yes / no* questions and three *Wh-*
questions in the simple past. Then share your questions with the class.

Example

Did Charles and Anne Lindbergh have any children?

1. _____

2. _____

3. _____

Example

Why did Lindbergh enter Orteig's contest?

4. _____

5. _____

6. _____

■■■■■■■■■■ **GO TO** MyEnglishLab **FOR MORE GRAMMAR PRACTICE AND TO CHECK WHAT YOU LEARNED.**

FINAL WRITING TASK

In this unit, you read about Charles Lindbergh and his first solo, non-stop flight across the Atlantic Ocean. You also read about Captain Chesley "Sully" Sullenberger, who safely landed his plane on the Hudson River and saved the lives of the people on board.

Now you are going to **write a narrative paragraph about a trip or adventure.** You can write about your own experience or that of another person. Use the vocabulary and grammar from this unit.*

PREPARE TO WRITE: Brainstorming

To help you write about your trip or adventure, you are going to brainstorm ideas. When you brainstorm, you think of as many ideas as possible. Then you make a list of your ideas.

1 Brainstorm a list of trips or adventures you had. Think of experiences with your family, friends, or classmates. Then think about *Wh-* questions for more ideas on that topic.

Examples

- Drove my father's car without asking and had an accident
- Took a road trip across the United States with friends
- Went hiking in the mountains and got lost
- Lost my wallet while traveling
- Went skydiving for the first time

2 Think about the experience you chose in Exercise 1. Add more details to help you write later.

Example

Took a road trip across the United States with friends / saw many fun things / car broke down[1]

Wh- Questions	Notes
Who?	Jenny, Lisa, Jackie—my classmates
When?	Three years ago
Where?	Visited cities, states, and national parks across the United States—driving east to west and then back
Why?	We wanted adventure. It was our dream to do it.
How?	In Lisa's car
How many?	Three people, 10 states
How much?	Cheap hotels, expensive to fix the car

---

[1] **broke down:** stopped working

* For Alternative Writing Topics, see page 145. These topics can be used in place of the writing topic for this unit or as homework. The alternative topics relate to the theme of the unit, but may not target the same grammar or rhetorical structures taught in the unit.

WH- QUESTIONS	NOTES
WHO?	
WHAT?	
WHEN?	
WHERE?	
WHY?	
HOW?	
HOW MANY?	
HOW MUCH?	

Note: You don't have to answer every question when brainstorming.

WRITE: Writing a Narrative Paragraph

A **narrative** is a story about an event or experience. The writer tells the story in time order starting with the first event and ending with the last event.

1 Read the sentences. Then put them in order. Number them from 1 to 8.

On Saturday, I went dancing with my friends. . . .

_____ At 12:00 A.M., I said good night to my friends, and I walked to the Metro.

_____ At 7:00 A.M., the Metro opened again. I got on. This time I did not fall asleep.

_____ I got on the train, I sat down, and I fell asleep. I was so tired from dancing.

_____ I left the train, and I walked out of the Metro. I was totally lost!

_____ Then I looked at my watch. It was after 3:00 A.M. No more trains!

__1__ We danced for three hours.

_____ When I woke up, someone was saying, "Get up! Last Stop!"

_____ I had no money for a taxi, so I went to a 24-hour coffee shop to wait for the Metro to open.

2 Now write the sentences in paragraph form in your notebook. Be sure to indent your paragraph.

3 Look at the timeline and complete the paragraph. Use past verb forms.

Our Weekend in Toronto

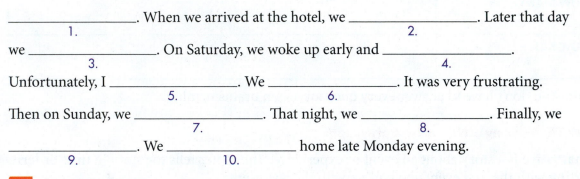

←FRIDAY -------------------- SATURDAY ----------------- SUNDAY ----------------- MONDAY→

• fly from Philadelphia to Toronto	• walk around the city	• buy gifts for friends	• get home
• take a nap	• lose wallet and passport	• have special dinner to celebrate our trip	
• visit with family / friend sat night	• spend rest of day trying to get them back	• pack our suitcases	

Last year, my friend and I took a weekend trip to Canada. On Friday, we

_____. When we arrived at the hotel, we _____. Later that day
     1.   2.

we _____. On Saturday, we woke up early and _____.
     3.   4.

Unfortunately, I _____. We _____. It was very frustrating.
                      5.   6.

Then on Sunday, we _____. That night, we _____. Finally, we
                       7.   8.

_____. We _____ home late Monday evening.
     9.   10.

4 Now write the first draft of your narrative paragraph about your trip or adventurous experience. Think about your answers to the *Wh-* questions in Exercise 2.

REVISE

USING TIME ORDER WORDS

Time order words show the order of events in a narrative. They help your reader understand your story. Time order words often come at the beginning of a sentence.

Example

I went to the beach with my brothers last week. **First**, we just sat on the beach. **Then** we went swimming in the ocean. **Next**, we played football in the sand. **Finally**, after three hours, we went home.

Other time words or expressions tell when or how long:

A specific day
On Wednesday, we flew to Boston. (*on Tuesday, on Friday, on Saturday*)

In the past
Last year, I went to London. (*last week, last month, yesterday*)
I went to Sydney **two years ago**. (*two months ago, two weeks ago, two days ago*)

In the future

We left **the next day**. (*the next week, the next month, the next year*)

We arrived in Florida on Tuesday. **Five days later**, we went to Georgia. (*three hours later, a year later*)

A period of time

We went to Florida **for a week**. (*for an hour, for a month, for a year*)

Note: Use time order words and expressions to make your writing clear for your reader. Don't use them in every sentence.

1 Look back at the paragraph about the trip to Toronto in the Write section, Exercise 3, on page 142. Underline the time order words or other time words.

2 Read the timeline below. Then choose the time expression that best completes each sentence. Write the correct time expression on the line.

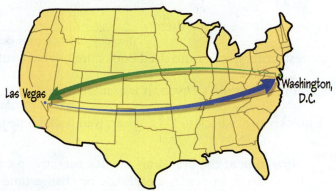

Monday, June 6	-Left Washington, D.C. -Drove towards Las Vegas, Nevada -Stopped in Bedford, Pennsylvania
Monday, June 13	-Arrived in Las Vegas
Tuesday, June 14	-Left Las Vegas -Drove towards Flagstaff, Arizona -Car broke down 10 miles before Flagstaff
Wednesday, June 15	-Stayed in Flagstaff
Thursday, June 16	-The Grand Canyon
Friday, June 17	-Flagstaff
Sunday, June 19	-Left Flagstaff
Tuesday, June 21	-Arrived back in Washington, D.C.

(continued on next page)

THE ROAD TRIP

_____Three years ago_____, my friends and I drove across the United States. It was an
      1. (Three years ago / First)

unforgettable adventure. _____, June 6th, we left Washington, D.C. and
      2. (For a week / On Monday)

drove west towards Las Vegas, Nevada. We drove _____. While driving,
      3. (five years later / for six days)

we stopped at many beautiful small towns, big cities, and national parks, but we got very tired

of driving. _____, on Monday, June 13th, we arrived at Las Vegas, Nevada. This was
      4. (Finally / First)

our last stop going west. We walked around the streets and looked at all the lights and people.

_____, on Tuesday, we began driving east again. _____,
5. (The next day / The day before)   6. (Then / Finally)

something terrible happened. Our car broke down near Flagstaff, Arizona. Flagstaff was not in

our plans, but we stayed there _____. Flagstaff is a nice town with many
      7. (two days ago / for five days)

nice restaurants, cafes, and used bookstores. What a surprise! We took small trips near Flagstaff,

including the Grand Canyon. It was amazing! _____, our car was ready.
      8. (Five days ago / Five days later)

We quickly drove back to D.C. We arrived back home in D.C. _____.
      9. (on Tuesday / two months ago)

3 Now look at the first draft of your narrative paragraph. Underline the time order words.
Is the order of events clear? Add or change time order words if needed.

▪▪▪▪▪▪▪▪▪▪▪▪▪▪▪▪▪▪▪▪▪▪▪▪▪▪▪▪▪▪ *GO TO* MyEnglishLab *FOR MORE SKILL PRACTICE.*

EDIT: Writing the Final Draft

Go to MYENGLISHLAB and write the final draft of your paragraph. Check your grammar,
spelling, capitalization, and punctuation. Check that you used some of the grammar and
vocabulary from the unit. Use the checklist to help you write your final draft. Then give your
paragraph to your teacher.

FINAL DRAFT CHECKLIST

❏ Did you write a narrative paragraph?

❏ Did you begin with a good topic sentence?

❏ Did you use vocabulary from the unit?

❏ Did you use simple past verbs?

❏ Did you put your ideas in a time order?

❏ Did you use time order words and expressions?

UNIT PROJECT

Work alone or with a partner. Choose a person from the list below, or think of another person who had an unforgettable trip or adventure. Collect information about this person and pictures, if possible. Follow the steps:

- Felix Baumgartner
- Laura Dekker
- Diana Nyad
- Sally Ride
- Aron Ralston

STEP 1: Look on the Internet for information about this person. Include pictures.

STEP 2: Make a list of events related to the trip or adventurous experience. Put the events in time order.

STEP 3: Write a paragraph of five to eight sentences about this person. Use simple past verbs. Begin your paragraph like this: _____ [name] had a very _____ [adjective] trip/experience.

ALTERNATIVE WRITING TOPICS

Write about one of the topics. Use grammar and vocabulary from this unit.

1. Interview someone you know about a trip or adventure they had. Write a narrative paragraph about that experience. Use the simple past.

2. The artist Andy Warhol said that everyone has "15 minutes of fame." That is, everyone becomes famous for a short time. Write a paragraph about someone you know who became famous for a short time. What happened? Did the person change? Use simple past verbs and time order words and expressions.

GO TO MyEnglishLab *TO WRITE ABOUT ONE OF THE ALTERNATIVE TOPICS, WATCH A VIDEO ABOUT A HEROIC PILOT, AND TAKE THE UNIT 6 ACHIEVEMENT TEST.*

WHAT NUMBER ARE
You?

1 FOCUS ON THE TOPIC

1. How many brothers and sisters are there in this family?

2. Do you have any brothers or sisters? If so, how many?

3. What is a good number of siblings to have? 0? 1? More?

GO TO MyEnglishLab *TO CHECK WHAT YOU KNOW.*

VOCABULARY

1 Read the sentences. Pay attention to the boldfaced words.

1. My friend Kam has ten **siblings**. He is the 11th child in his family.

2. David studied hard for the test. He is **likely** to do well on it.

3. My parents **expect** me to go to college after high school, but I want to travel for a year.

4. My little sister is really **spoiled**. My parents give her everything she wants. She never says thank you. She just wants more and more.

5. Even "good" kids **misbehave** sometimes. No child is good all the time.

6. People say all Asians are good at math, but that is just a **stereotype**. I'm Asian, but I'm not good at math.

7. My parents had many **rules**. One was to do my homework right after school.

8. When I was young, my parents were very **strict** with me. I had to go home after school to do my homework. Also, I had to go to bed at 8:00 P.M.

9. In my family, there are three kids. My sister is the oldest, I am the **middle** child, and my brother is the youngest.

10. Polly was **born** in Boston, but she now lives in Philadelphia.

2 Match the definitions with the boldfaced words above. Write the number of the sentence on the line.

_____ probably, almost certainly

_____ brothers and sisters

_____ behaving badly because you get too much money or attention, or too many things

_____ in between two people or things

_____ starting life, coming out of your mother's body

_____ to think something will or should happen in the future

_____ making sure rules are followed

_____ to behave or act badly

_____ an idea about a particular type of person which is wrong or unfair

_____ what you can and cannot do

GO TO MyEnglishLab **FOR MORE VOCABULARY PRACTICE.**

PREVIEW

Read about John Ichikawa. Then decide if he is the oldest, middle, or youngest child in his family. Choose one. Explain your answer to a partner.

John Ichikawa is a medical doctor in Chicago. He is very successful and respected in the community. He is married and has two children. They live in a nice house. His parents live nearby. John sees his parents often and gives them money every month. They go on vacations with John and his family.

I think John Ichikawa is probably the _____ child in his family because
(oldest / middle / youngest)
_____.

Now read a section from a textbook about families.

TIMING IS EVERYTHING

1   Members of the same family have similarities. However, research shows that there are differences among oldest, **middle**, and youngest children. Scientists want to know: What are the differences and where do they come from?

The First Born

2   Oldest children are often very responsible[1] and organized. The reason is the parents. Parents **expect** the oldest child to be an example for the younger children to follow.

3   First-**born** children are often more educated than younger **siblings**. As a result, firstborns are more **likely** to have high-paying jobs. They become CEOs and doctors.

4   Firstborns get a lot of attention from their parents at an early age. However, they also have more **rules** to follow than younger children. For example, they have an early bedtime. New parents are usually **strict** with their first child.

_____

[1] **responsible:** behaving in a sensible way and can be trusted

(continued on next page)

The Middle Child

5   Middle children do not have the benefits of the oldest child. They also do not have the freedom of the youngest. Unlike the oldest and youngest, middle children are never alone in the family. They have to share their parents' time, attention, or money with other siblings.

6   Middle children have to work harder to get attention. Sometimes they feel left out, so they **misbehave** to get attention. They are called the "problem children." Also, they might look outside the family to get attention or to feel special.

7   Middle children are often independent. They are good at solving[2] problems. They can get help from the oldest, but they can also help the youngest. However, middle children often go to their friends for advice, not to their parents or siblings.

The Baby

8   When the third child arrives, parents are usually more confident[3] but less energetic than before. As a result, the youngest child often has more freedom. Bedtimes are later. Parents are also more generous with their money. The baby usually gets what he or she wants. This is a problem if the child becomes **spoiled**.

9   Last-born children are often more adventurous. They are more likely to take risks. They play risky sports such as ice hockey or football. The youngest is also more likely to be an artist, a firefighter, or an independent business owner.

10   They are also funny. When you are the little one, older siblings will be nice to you if you make them laugh.

11   Some people think that parents cause the personality differences in their children. Other people say these birth order descriptions are not true; they are just **stereotypes**. Of course, every family is different. However, studying birth order may help us understand families.

---

[2] **solving:** finding the answer
[3] **confident:** feeling sure that you can do something well

MAIN IDEAS

1 Look again at your prediction in the Preview section on page 149. Did your prediction match the information in the reading?

2 Read each sentence. Choose the main idea in the reading. Put a check (✓).

_____ **1.** People agree that birth order stereotypes are true.

_____ **2.** There is a connection between birth order and personality.

_____ **3.** Birth order differences come only from the parents.

DETAILS

According to the reading, do these words and phrases describe the first-born (1), middle (2), or last-born (3) child in a family? Write the number on the line.

_____ adventurous   _____ funny   _____ left out

_____ oldest   _____ organized   _____ "problem child"

_____ problem solver   _____ responsible   _____ spoiled

_____ youngest   _____ more educated _____ independent

MAKE INFERENCES

RECOGNIZING COMPARISONS

An **inference** is an "**educated**" **guess** about something. The information is **not stated directly** in the reading.

Writers often make **comparisons**—show how two things are the same or different. Sometimes these comparisons are not always directly stated. You have to make inferences to understand the comparisons.

A comparison sentence usually has two parts.

     #1   #2

First-born children are often **more educated than** younger siblings. (paragraph 3)

A writer may not always include the second part (#2).

Look at the same comparison with only one part. As a reader, you have to infer the second part of the sentence to understand the comparison.

     #1   #2

First-born children are often **more educated**. (**than** younger siblings)

Can you infer the second part of this example?

                               #1

New parents are usually **strict** with their first child. (paragraph 4)

You can infer that the writer is comparing first-born children to later-born children. Here is the sentence with both parts:

                                #1   #2

New parents are usually **stricter** with their first-born child **than with their later-born children**.

Answer each question with a comparison. Use the boldfaced words in your answers. Look at the paragraphs in parentheses. Answers may vary.

1. Who has **higher-paying jobs**? (paragraph 3)

   _____Firstborn children have higher-paying jobs than the younger siblings._____

2. Who has to **work harder to get attention**? (paragraph 6)

   _____

3. Who is **more adventurous**? (paragraph 9)

   _____

4. Who is **more likely to be a firefighter**? (paragraph 9)

   _____

EXPRESS OPINIONS

Read Reading One again. Then think about the first-born, middle-born, or last-born children in your family (or a family you know). Does the research on birth order seem true to you? Complete the statements to answer the question and explain why.

Example

I don't think the research on last-born children is true. In my family I am the youngest. I am responsible. I am not spoiled.

1. I think the research on _____ -born children is true. In my family
   (first / middle / last)

   _____.

2. I'm not so sure the research on _____ -born children is true. In my family
   (first / middle / last)

   _____.

3. I don't think the research on _____ -born children is true. In my family
   (first / middle / last)

   _____.

■■■■■■■■■■■■■■■■■■■■■■■■■■■■ *GO TO* MyEnglishLab *TO GIVE YOUR OPINION ABOUT ANOTHER QUESTION.*

READ

1 Look at the boldfaced words in the reading and think about the questions.

1. Which of these words do you know?

2. What do the words mean?

2 A case study is a long, descriptive example. Read this case study from a sociology textbook. As you read, notice the boldfaced words. Try to guess the meaning from the context.

CASE STUDY: THE KOH FAMILY

1   Vincent and Helen Koh live in Arcadia, California. They have three children. They are all **adults** now.

2   Ellen, the oldest, lives in Arcadia. In fact, Ellen and her parents are next-door **neighbors**. Unfortunately, she does not see her parents often. She is the busy mother of three daughters. She is the CEO of the Arcadia Savings Bank. She also volunteers twice a week at the local hospital. These are only three of her responsibilities.

3   The Koh's middle child, Tim, lives in Los Angeles, about an hour away from his parents. He visits often and helps them with their computer problems. Tim is married to Sally. Their son, Steven, is in high school. Tim stays home and takes care of his family. He works part-time selling houses. Tim loves risky sports. He plays ice hockey once a week. Tim, his wife, and his son go skiing almost every weekend in the winter.

4   Jeff is the youngest. He is the "baby," but he is almost 40 years old. He lives in Philadelphia far away from his parents. Jeff got his Ph.D. in biology, and he is now a university professor. Like his sister, he also volunteers at a hospital. On weekends he performs[1] in a comedy club. He enjoys it. When he was young, he always made his family laugh. Now people pay him to be funny.

---

[1] **perform:** to do something to entertain people

COMPREHENSION

Read each statement. Write **T** (true) or **F** (false). If the statement is false, change one word to make it true.

_____ **1.** Vincent and Helen Koh have 4 grandchildren.

_____ **2.** Ellen is a CEO at a hospital.

_____ **3.** Tim lives with his family in Philadelphia.

_____ **4.** Tim enjoys sports.

_____ **5.** Jeff is the first-born child in this family.

■■■■■■■■■■■■■■■■■■■■■■■■■■ **GO TO** MyEnglishLab **FOR MORE VOCABULARY PRACTICE.**

READING SKILL

1 Look at Reading Two again. Then read the sentences. Choose the word or phrase from the box that means the same as the underlined word.

Ellen's	doing stand-up comedy	Tim and Sally's
Tim, Sally, and Steve	~~Vincent and Helen Koh~~	being a parent, a CEO, and a volunteer

1. <u>They</u> have three adult children. (paragraph 1) _____ *Vincent and Helen Koh* _____

2. Ellen and <u>her</u> parents are next-door neighbors. (paragraph 2) _____

3. <u>These</u> are only three of her responsibilities. (paragraph 2) _____

4. <u>Their</u> son, Steven, is in high school. (paragraph 3) _____

5. <u>They</u> all go skiing almost every weekend in the winter. (paragraph 3) _____

6. He enjoys <u>it</u>. (paragraph 4) _____

UNDERSTANDING WORD REFERENCE

A noun names a person, place, thing, or idea. A pronoun is a word that takes the place of a noun.

When you read, it is important to connect pronouns to the correct noun. Understanding these connections can help you understand what you read.

Sometimes the pronoun refers to a noun in the same sentence. Other times the pronoun refers to a noun in an earlier sentence.

Subject pronouns: *I, you, he, she, it, we, they*

For example:
They have three adult children. (*They* refers to *Vincent and Helen Koh.*)
They all go skiing almost every weekend in the winter. (*They* refers to *Tim, Sally, and Steve.*)

Object pronouns: *me, you, him, her, us, them*

For example:
He enjoys it. (*It* refers to *performing stand-up comedy.*)

There is also a connection between nouns and possessive adjectives (*my, your, his, her, its, our, their*)

For example:
Ellen and her parents are next-door neighbors. *(Her refers to Ellen.)*
Their son, Steven, is in high school. (*Their* refers to *Tim and Sally.*)

The words *this, that, these,* and *those* make connections to ideas stated before.

For example:
These are only three of her responsibilities. (*These* refers to *being a parent, a CEO, and a volunteer.*)

---

2 Look at Reading One again. Then read the sentences. Write the word or phrase that means the same as the underlined word. Use the paragraph numbers in parentheses to help you find the information.

1. This is because parents have high expectations. (paragraph 2)

    _____ *being responsible and organized* _____

2. They become CEOs and doctors. (paragraph 3) _____

3. New parents are usually strict with their first-born children. (paragraph 4)

    _____

4. Middle children may go to their friends for advice, not their parents. (paragraph 7)

    _____

5. The "baby" usually gets what he or she wants. (paragraph 8)

    _____

(continued on next page)

6. <u>This</u> is a problem if the child becomes spoiled. (paragraph 8) _____

7. <u>They</u> play risky sports like ice hockey or rugby. (paragraph 9) _____

8. Others see some truth in <u>them</u>. (paragraph 11) _____

GO TO MyEnglishLab *FOR MORE SKILL PRACTICE.*

CONNECT THE READINGS

STEP 1: Organize

Review the information of birth order in Reading One and the descriptions of the Koh children in Reading Two. Complete the chart. Then compare your answers with a partner.

IDEAS FROM READING ONE	IDEAS FROM READING TWO	
	TYPICAL	NOT TYPICAL
<u>The First Born</u> • responsible • organized • educated	*Ellen is the oldest.* *She is very responsible and organized.* *She is a CEO of a bank. I think she went to college.*	*Ellen . . .*
<u>The Middle Child</u> • independent • looks outside the family for attention • "problem child" • problem solver		
<u>The Baby</u> • adventurous • artistic • funny • spoiled		

STEP 2: Synthesize

Work with a partner. One partner is Vincent Koh and the other is Helen Koh. Think about how your children fit (or do not fit) the ideas in Reading One. Use the chart in Step 1. Complete the sentences. Write about all three of your children. Then discuss your ideas with your partner.

_____ fits the description of a _____ -born child. She/He
    (name)   (first / middle / last)

_____ .

_____ doesn't fit the description of a _____ -born child.
    (name)   (first / middle / last)

She/He _____ .

GO TO MyEnglishLab *TO CHECK WHAT YOU LEARNED.*

VOCABULARY

REVIEW

Complete the passage with the correct word from the box.

adults	confident	likely	misbehave	rules	stereotypes
born	~~expect~~	middle	neighbor	spoiled	strict

The Only-Child Syndrome

An only child is a person with no siblings. Some people think only children are selfish, lonely, or unhappy. They say it is difficult for an only child to play or work with others. This is called the "Only-Child Syndrome."

It is true that parents _____*expect*_____ a lot from their only child—similar to the
1.
oldest child in other families. Only-children are often very responsible. They are also better at communicating because they speak mostly with _____ at home.
2.

Like _____ children, only children are more _____ to make
3.   4.
friends outside the home. This is natural. They need to play with other kids.

Like the youngest children, only children may be a little _____ by their
5.
parents. They get 100 percent of their parents' time and attention.

Some parents are _____ —their children have to follow a lot of
6.
_____. But no child is good all the time. All children _____
7.   8.
sometimes.

(continued on next page)

Polly Hollingsworth is my next-door _____. We were also

9.

_____ on the same day. She is also an only child. Polly says that she was

10.

not lonely or unhappy. She doesn't fit the description of an only child. Today, Polly is very

_____. She can talk to people easily and she is not afraid of anything.

11.

Spoiled? Lonely? Unhappy? These may be _____. There is no big difference

12.

between only children and people with siblings. Only children are just like other children.

EXPAND

Read the idioms and expressions about families. Then complete the sentences with an idiom
or expression about family. Use the correct form of the verb.

sibling rivalry: competition between brothers and
   sisters in a family
the black sheep: the family member who has a different
   life from the others
raise a family/children: care for and give your children
   the things they need. Parents raise a family. They raise
   their children.
grow up: get older. Children grow up and become
   adults.
take after: be similar to an older family member, such as a parent or sibling
It runs in the family: All the family members have something in common, such as hair
   color or personality.

1. Everyone in my family went to college. They all work in offices, and they all live in the
   city. I decided not to go to college. I live on a farm. I am definitely _____ of the
   family.

2. Jane likes to play tennis. She _____ her father. He plays tennis often.

3. Mr. and Mrs. Sullivan were very friendly to their neighbors. Their children are friendly,
   too. Friendliness _____.

4. Patrick and Peter are twins. There is a lot of _____ between them. One is
   always trying to be better than the other in school and in sports.

5. You need a lot of money to _____. You need to pay for clothes, food, and
   school.

6. Raymond doesn't want to _____. He wants to be a teenager forever.

CREATE

In your notebook, write six sentences about your family. Use the words and phrases from the Review and Expand sections.

■■■■■■■■■■■■■■■■■■■■■■■ *GO TO* MyEnglishLab *FOR MORE VOCABULARY PRACTICE.*

GRAMMAR

1 Molly and Holly are sisters. Read the chart. Then answer the questions.

	MOLLY	**HOLLY**
YOUNG	is 25 years old	is 24 years old
TALL	is 5'2" tall (157 cm.)	is 5'7" tall (170 cm.)
FRIENDLY	is friendly	is a little shy
ATHLETIC	was in the Olympics once	watched the Olympics on TV once

1. Which sister is younger, Molly or Holly? _____Holly is younger than Molly (is)._____

2. Which sister is taller? _____

3. Who is friendlier? _____

4. Which one is more athletic? _____

COMPARATIVE ADJECTIVES

1. Use the comparative form of adjectives to compare two people, places, or things. Use ***than*** when you are comparing two things in a sentence.	Holly is **taller than** her sister, Molly. Molly is **more athletic than** Holly.
2. For adjectives with one syllable, add *-er* + ***than***. cool long old short shy strict tall young Notice the spelling change for adjectives that end in consonant-vowel-consonant: big → bigger thin → thinner	Molly is **shorter than** Holly. Holly is **younger than** Molly. Sydney is a big city. Tokyo is **bigger than** Sydney. Molly is **thinner than** Holly.

(continued on next page)

3. For adjectives with two or more syllables, use **more + adjective + than**. adventurous athletic boring exciting handsome interesting	Molly is **more intelligent than** Polly.
4. For adjectives with **two syllables** that end in -**y**, change the -**y** to -**i** and add -**er** + **than**. busy friendly funny risky heavy lucky wealthy	Molly is **friendlier than** Holly.
5. Some adjectives have irregular comparative forms. bad → **worse** *than* fun → **more fun** *than* good → **better** *than* likely → **more likely** *than* quiet → **quieter** *than* spoiled → **more spoiled** *than*	Holly is a **good** cook. Holly is a **better** cook **than** Molly (is).

2 Phil and Bill are brothers. Study the chart. Pay attention to how they are similar and different.

PHIL	BILL
is 38 years old	is 40 years old
is 5' 10" (178 cm)	is 6' (183 cm)
is average looking	is handsome
is a brain surgeon	is a teacher
works 14 hours a day	works 10 hours a day
makes $500,000 a year	makes $50,000 a year
drives a new Ferrari	drives an old Hyundai
enjoys watching TV	enjoys traveling and climbing mountains

3 Look at the information about Phil and Bill. Complete all the questions. Use the correct comparative form of the word in parentheses. Then, answer the questions.

1. Which brother is _____*taller*_____ (tall)? _____*Bill is taller than Phil.*_____

2. Which one is _*more handsome*_ (handsome)? _*Bill is more handsome than Phil.*_

3. Which one is _____ (good-looking)? _____

4. Which brother drives a _____ (cool) car? _____

5. Who is _____ (old)?   _____

6. Which brother is _____ (busy)?   _____

7. Which one is _____ (adventurous)?   _____

8. Which brother is _____ (interesting)?   _____

9. Which one has a _____ (exciting) life?   _____

10. Which is probably _____ (fun) to go on a date with? _____

4 Both Phil and Bill asked Jill on a date. She needs to choose. Which brother should Jill go out on a date with? Why? Write five sentences. Use comparative adjectives.

Jill should go out on a date with _____ *because . . . .*
   (Phil / Bill)

_____

_____

_____

_____

_____

■■■■■■■■■■■■■ *GO TO* MyEnglishLab *FOR MORE GRAMMAR PRACTICE AND TO CHECK WHAT YOU LEARNED.*

FINAL WRITING TASK

In this unit you read about stereotypes about birth order. You also read about the members of the Koh family.

Now you are going to **write a comparison paragraph about two family members.** They can be members of your family or another family. You will write about how they are similar or different. Use the vocabulary and grammar from the unit.*

PREPARE TO WRITE: Using a Venn diagram

A Venn diagram helps you to think about the similarities and differences between two things. In the center, you can list all the similarities. On the two sides, you can list the differences. The Venn diagram on page 163 describes Prince William and Prince Harry, pictured here.

---

* For Alternative Writing Topics, see page 169. These topics can be used in place of the writing topic for this unit or as homework. The alternative topics relate to the theme of the unit, but may not target the same grammar or rhetorical structures taught in the unit.

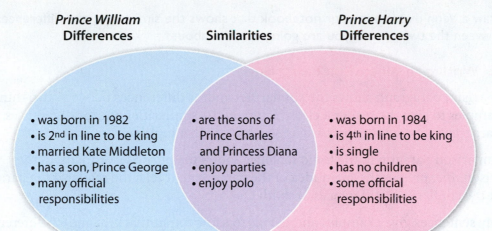

Prince William Differences

- was born in 1982
- is 2nd in line to be king
- married Kate Middleton
- has a son, Prince George
- many official responsibilities

Similarities

- are the sons of Prince Charles and Princess Diana
- enjoy parties
- enjoy polo

Prince Harry Differences

- was born in 1984
- is 4th in line to be king
- is single
- has no children
- some official responsibilities

The Venn diagram makes it easy to see the similarities and differences between the two brothers.

1 Look at the information about Ellen and Tim. Then complete the Venn diagram.

Ellen

- Has a full-time job
- Thinks family is important
- Has three daughters
- Takes them to soccer and dance
- Spends time with them on weekends
- Eats out with them

Tim

- Has a part-time job
- Thinks family is important
- Has one son and wife
- Runs and skis with his family
- Spends time with his family on weekends
- Cooks and eats at home

Ellen Differences   **Similarities**   **Tim Differences**

_____   _____   _____
_____   _____   _____
_____   _____   _____
_____   _____   _____

Draw a Venn diagram in your notebook that shows the similarities and differences between the two people you are going to write about.

WRITE: Writing a Comparison Paragraph

A **comparison** paragraph shows the similarities and/or differences between two things. It uses examples to give the reader a clear picture of the similarities and/or differences. Like other paragraphs, a comparison paragraph begins with a topic sentence.

In a comparison paragraph, the topic sentence shows the purpose, or focus, of the comparison. It expresses the main idea of the paragraph. It tells the reader if the paragraph is about the similarities, differences, or both.

The body sentences give examples and details to show the similarities and/or differences. These details focus on specific **points of comparison** between the two things or people.

Example

> Ellen and Tim are siblings, but their weekly routines[1] are very different. Ellen has a full-time job. After work and on weekends, Ellen watches her daughters' soccer games or takes them to dance lessons. Ellen and her daughters often eat out during the week. On Saturday nights, they also like to make popcorn and watch movies. Unlike Ellen, Tim only works part-time, so he spends time with his son every afternoon. They like to run together. Every weekend they do things together. For example, they go skiing or play sports. Similar to Ellen, Tim has dinner with his family every night. He cooks, and they eat together at home. Ellen and Tim are very busy, but they spend their time in different ways.

The main idea of this paragraph is that Ellen and Tim do different things with their families. In this paragraph, the writer makes a **block comparison** between Ellen and Tim. First, he decides what he wants to compare—his **points of comparison**: their *work* and *activities*. Then he writes about each point of comparison—first about Ellen and then about Tim. The writer concludes the paragraph by returning to the main idea of the paragraph.

---

[1] **routines:** regular way of doing things

1 Read the paragraph about Ellen and Tim again. Then look at the words and phrases in the box. Complete the outline. Fill in the topic sentence and the points of comparison. Use the words in the box.

activities	cooking and eating at home
eating out	full-time job
part-time job	running and skiing
taking the kids to soccer and dance	watching movies and having popcorn
work	

Topic sentence: _____

A. Ellen

   1. Work: _____

   2. Activities

     a) _____

     b) _____

     c) _____

B. Tim

   1. _____

   2. _____

     a) _____

     b) _____

2 Work with a partner. Look at the topic sentence below, and then look at the Venn diagram about Princes William and Harry on page 163. Choose two or three points of comparison together. Fill in the outline for a comparison paragraph. Then complete the paragraph about Princes William and Harry on your own in your notebook. Use the topic sentence below to begin your paragraph.

Topic sentence: *Princes William and Harry have many similarities, but, as they get*

        older, their lives are more different.

(continued on next page)

A. Prince William

1. _____

2. _____

3. _____

B. Prince Harry

1. _____

2. _____

3. _____

3 Write the topic sentence of your paragraph about two family members. Be sure that it states the focus of your comparison.

4 Now write the first draft of your comparison paragraph. Start with your topic sentence. Then write sentences that give details and examples about the points you are comparing. Finish your paragraph with a concluding sentence.

REVISE: Connecting words to show similarity and difference

These words and phrases will help you connect ideas in your paragraph. Use a comma after each of these phrases.

SIMILARITY	DIFFERENCE
Similar to (name), Like (name),	In contrast to (name), Unlike (name),
Examples	

Examples

Like Ellen, her parents live in Arcadia California. (They all live in the same city.)
Similar to Ellen, Tim has dinner with his family every night. (They both have dinner with their families but in different ways.)

Unlike most middle children, Tim enjoys playing risky sports.
In contrast to Ellen, who works in a bank, Tim works part-time selling houses.

Note that *like* means "almost exactly the same." *Similar to* is less specific. It does not mean "the same as."

1 Look at the chart. Complete the sentences with the correct names.

	MOLLY	HOLLY	POLLY
YOUNG	is 25 years old	is 24 years old.	is 24 years old
TALL	is 5′2″ (157 cm)	is 5′7″ (170 cm)	is 5′2″ (157 cm)
FRIENDLY	is friendly	is a little shy	is friendly
ATHLETIC	was in the Olympics once	watched the Olympics on TV once	was in the Olympics twice
BUSY	works 20 hours a week	works 40 hours a week and goes to school	relaxes most days

1. Like _____Molly_____, _____ is 5′2″ tall.

2. In contrast to _____, who works a lot, _____ isn't very busy.

3. Unlike _____ and _____, _____ is 5′7″.

4. Unlike her two sisters, _____ isn't very athletic.

5. Similar to her sister Molly, _____ is friendly.

2 Write sentences about the three brothers. Use the information in the chart. Then compare your sentences with a partner.

PHIL	BILL	GIL
is 38 years old	is 40 years old	is 38 years old
is 5′ 10″ (178 cm)	is 6′ (183 cm)	is 5′ 10″ (178 cm)
is average looking	is handsome	is not good-looking
is a brain surgeon	is a teacher	is a CEO
works 14 hours a day	works 10 hours a day	works 12 hours a day
makes $500,000 a year	makes $50,000 a year	makes $350,000 a year
drives a new Ferrari	drives an old Hyundai	drives a 2015 Ford
enjoys watching TV	enjoys traveling and climbing mountains	enjoys rap music & poetry

1. (Like / be 5′10″ tall) _____ Like Phil, Gil is 5′10″ tall. _____

2. (Similar to / make a lot of money) _____

3. (In contrast to / drive a cool car) _____

(continued on next page)

4. (Like / be . . . years old) _____

5. (Your idea) _____

3 Now look at the first draft of your paragraph. Add connecting words to show similarity and differences.

■■■■■■■■■■■■■■■■■■■■■■■■■■■■■■■■■■■■ *GO TO* MyEnglishLab *FOR MORE SKILL PRACTICE.*

EDIT: Writing the Final Draft

Go to MYENGLISHLAB and write the final draft of your paragraph. Check your grammar, spelling, capitalization, and punctuation. Check that you used some of the grammar and vocabulary from the unit. Use the checklist to help you write your final draft. Then give your paragraph to your teacher.

FINAL DRAFT CHECKLIST

❏ Did you write a comparison paragraph about two members of a family?

❏ Did you use a topic sentence?

❏ Did you use vocabulary from the unit?

❏ Did you have clear points of comparison?

❏ Did you use correct comparative forms?

❏ Did you use connecting words to show similarities and differences?

UNIT PROJECT

Work alone or with a partner. Research a famous family, such as a royal family, a famous family of actors, or a family on television. Follow these steps.

STEP 1: Brainstorm a list of famous families you know. Choose one to research.

STEP 2: Search online for information and pictures about this family. Read and take notes. Include important ideas such as names, ages, and important events in the family's life.

STEP 3: Write two paragraphs. First, describe the family in general. Who are they? Where are they from? Why are they famous? Second, write a paragraph about how two members of the family are similar or different.

STEP 4: Present your research to the class. Show pictures as you talk about the family.

ALTERNATIVE WRITING TOPICS

Write about one of the topics. Use grammar and vocabulary from this unit.

1. Do you believe the ideas about birth order are true? Write a paragraph with your opinion.

2. The research on birth order talks about families with two or three children. Do you think the results are different if there are *more* than three children (or fewer than three) in a family? Write a paragraph.

3. We all know people that we *think of* as family, but who are not really our family. Write a paragraph about someone who is "like family" to you.

■■■■■■■■■■■■■■■■■■■■■■■ *GO TO* MyEnglishLab *TO WRITE ABOUT ONE OF THE ALTERNATIVE TOPICS,*
WATCH A VIDEO ABOUT BIRTH ORDER AND YOUR HEALTH, AND TAKE THE UNIT 7 ACHIEVEMENT TEST. ■■■■■■■■■■■

HOW YOUNG IS TOO Young?

1 FOCUS ON THE TOPIC

1. What is happening in the picture?

2. What sports do you like to play or watch? What do you like about them?

3. What are the benefits of being a professional athlete[1]? What are some of the drawbacks?

_____

[1] **professional athlete:** someone who is paid to play a sport

GO TO MyEnglishLab **TO CHECK WHAT YOU KNOW.**

VOCABULARY

 1 Read about three young athletes. Pay attention to the boldfaced words.

Most soccer fans say that Brazil's Pelé was the greatest soccer player ever. He showed his **talent** for soccer at a young age. In 1958, when he was just 17 years old, Pelé became the youngest player to win the World Cup with his team. In his career, Pelé has had to **deal with** many challenges: being an athlete, being a media star, and being a role model for kids.

In 1997, at the age of 17, Martina Hingis became the youngest #1 women's tennis player. She was a great athlete, but she was not a **mature** woman yet. Martina made some **comments** about other players. For example, in 1998, she called another tennis player "old and slow." Later, her comments were much more **responsible**. When she was 22, Hingis had **difficulties** with her legs and had to stop playing tennis. She started playing again when she was 25 but retired[1] at age 27.

Michele Wie became a professional golfer long before she **graduated** from high school. She **earned** over $10 million in her first year. She was 15 years old. Wie was good enough to play professional men's golf. But her **coach** told her that she should continue to play women's golf.

---

[1] **retired:** stopped working

2 Match the words on the left with the definitions on the right.

___h___ **1.** talent   **a.** taking care of others and doing what you say you will do

_____ **2.** mature   **b.** problems

_____ **3.** comments   **c.** received money for doing something

_____ **4.** responsible   **d.** grown up, like an adult

_____ **5.** difficulties   **e.** finished education at a school

_____ **6.** earned   **f.** try to handle a difficulty in the correct way

_____ **7.** graduated   **g.** a person who teaches a sport

_____ **8.** coach   **h.** ~~natural ability to do something like art, music, or sports~~

_____ **9.** deal with   **i.** ideas a person says or writes about something or someone

■■■■■■■■■■■■■■■■■■■■■■■■■■■■■■■■■ **GO TO** MyEnglishLab **FOR MORE VOCABULARY PRACTICE.**

PREVIEW

Read the title of the newspaper article. Before you read, think about what the title might mean. What ideas do you think you will read about Ronnie in the article? Check (✓) your ideas.

_____ **1.** He is going to change his name.

_____ **2.** He is going to move to another country.

_____ **3.** He is going to become a professional baseball player.

_____ **4.** He is going to go to college.

Now read the newspaper article about a special young athlete.

The Metropolitan Herald

July 23, 2013

Ready Ronnie?

by Richard Gray

1   IN A FEW DAYS, he will be a professional baseball player. Ronnie Elkhouly will **earn** about $600,000 per year. Nike® will pay him about $2 million to wear their shoes and clothes. That is more than most other U.S. professional baseball players earn today. But right now, Elkhouly needs to finish high school.

2   Ronnie Elkhouly is 16 years old, and he attends the Brock Educational Institute. Brock is a school for students with special **talents** in sports or art. Many of them, like Elkhouly, **graduate** from high school early. At Brock, Elkhouly learns about math and English. Elkhouly and the other students also learn how to **deal with** living in the spotlight.[1]

3   There is a whole team of teachers and **coaches** helping Elkhouly to prepare for the professional world. They gave him a job at a preschool.[2] They say that taking care of three-year-olds will teach Elkhouly to be **responsible**. He will need to be responsible in the difficult world of professional sports. His coaches talk to him about the **difficulties** of being famous. For example, sometimes the media say unkind or untrue things about athletes. "People will say that Elkhouly is not **mature**. They will talk about his family. They will say he makes too much money," says one of Elkhouly's coaches. The coaches help Elkhouly understand that he cannot get angry about these **comments**.

4   Elkhouly also gets support from older professional athletes, like Wayne Tothrow from the Las Vegas Rattlesnakes football team.

Tothrow told Elkhouly, "Go out and have fun, but take care of yourself." Tothrow also told him to be careful. He said that people— even your family and friends— can sometimes change when you have a lot of money. "Ronnie listens. He asks questions," Tothrow said.

5   In a few days, life will change forever for Elkhouly. He will graduate from Brock and enter the world of professional baseball. The teachers at Brock think that 16-year-old Elkhouly is mature enough to play pro baseball. But there is no test for maturity[3] at school. The real test will begin after he graduates.

---

[1] **in the spotlight:** famous; seen or watched by the public
[2] **preschool:** a school for children under six years old
[3] **maturity:** being mature

MAIN IDEAS

1 Look again at your predictions in the Preview section on page 173. Circle your predictions that match information from the reading.

2 Check (✓) the answer that includes the most important points in the article.

_____ **1.** Ronnie's teachers and coaches give him advice about the difficulties of being a pro athlete. For example, professional athletes' families sometimes want to take their money.

_____ **2.** Ronnie Elkhouly will soon become a pro baseball player. He is young, so his teachers and coaches want to prepare him for the professional world. No one thinks he is mature enough to play pro.

_____ **3.** Ronnie Elkhouly is young, but his teachers and coaches are helping him become mature very fast. They are not worried about him going into the professional baseball world. However, some people think it's a bad idea.

DETAILS

Circle the best answer to complete each statement.

1. Ronnie Elkhouly will earn _____ some older professional athletes.

    a. less than

    b. the same as

    c. more than

2. Brock is a school for _____.

    a. professional baseball players

    b. baseball and soccer coaches

    c. talented young athletes

3. One difficulty for professional athletes is _____.

    a. taking care of small children

    b. being in the spotlight

    c. taking tests

4. The coaches at Brock are helping Elkhouly learn to _____.

    a. deal with people's comments

    b. earn a lot of money

    c. take care of his family

(continued on next page)

5. The coaches and teachers at Brock think that Elkhouly is _____.

    a. too young to play professional baseball

    b. strong enough to play for the Las Vegas Rattlesnakes

    c. ready to become a professional athlete

MAKE INFERENCES

UNDERSTANDING PEOPLE'S PRIORITIES

An **inference** is an **"educated" guess** about something. The information is **not stated directly** in the reading. Writers sometimes suggest people's **priorities** without directly stating them. Priorities are the things that are most important to a person (or group of people). Often, people's priorities are their reasons for doing things.

  Read paragraph one again. What is Nike's priority?

  a. to use Elkhouly to earn money
  b. to give advice about being famous
  c. to say negative things about Elkhouly
  d. to help Elkhouly be careful about other people
  e. to teach Elkhouly about math and other school subjects

From paragraph 1, we know that Nike will pay Ronnie Elkhouly a lot of money to wear their shoes and clothes. Also, we understand that Nike is a company. Companies earn money when a famous person wears their products.

The best answer is **a. We can infer that** Nike's priority is to make money.

What priorities do these people (or groups of people) have? Choose what is most important for each person (or group of people). Refer to the paragraphs in parentheses.

   _a_ **1.** Nike™ (paragraph 1)   ~~**a.** to use Elkhouly to earn money~~

   ____ **2.** Brock coaches (paragraph 3)   **b.** to give advice about being famous

   ____ **3.** Wayne Tothrow (paragraph 4)   **c.** to say negative things about Elkhouly

   ____ **4.** Brock teachers (paragraphs 1, 2)   **d.** to help Elkhouly be careful about other people

   ____ **5.** the media (paragraph 3)   **e.** to teach Elkhouly about math and other school subjects

EXPRESS OPINIONS

Check (✓) the box that matches your opinion. Then discuss your answers with a partner. Give reasons and ask questions.

	I AGREE.	IT DEPENDS.	I DISAGREE.
1. Age 16 is too young to become a professional athlete.			
2. You can't learn how to be responsible in school.			
3. $600,000 a year is too much money for a 16-year-old to earn.			

■■■■■■■■■■■■■■■■■■■■■■■ *GO TO* MyEnglishLab *TO GIVE YOUR OPINION ABOUT ANOTHER QUESTION.*

READING TWO   EVAN BURCH

READ

1 Look at the boldfaced words and phrases in the reading on page 178 and think about the questions.

1. Which of these words do you know?

2. What do the words mean?

EVAN BURCH: YOUNG BASKETBALL STAR SAYS "NO" TO THE PROS

Interview by Nicola Quinn

You probably don't know Evan Burch—not yet. But basketball coaches know him, and they think he has a lot of talent. He is a college basketball star. At 18 years old and after graduating from high school, Evan Burch is now old enough to join a professional basketball team, but the NBA[1] will have to wait. Burch wants to graduate from college first.

NQ: Evan, everyone expected you to join the NBA this year. Why did you decide to finish college first?

EB: Well, I planned to join the NBA as soon as I was old enough. But then I met older basketball players. They **recommended** that I stay in college.

NQ: Who did you talk to?

EB: Several basketball players. But Kwasi Rodland probably helped me the most. He is my biggest basketball hero. He's the greatest. He retired in 1990. He played pro basketball for 20 years, so he has a lot of **experience**. But, in his day, all players had to go to college before joining the NBA. Today it's different. He said college helped the players to become more mature—intellectually and physically.

NQ: But what about the money? How can you say "no" to all that money?

EB: Oh, that was really hard! On the wall in my bedroom, I had photos of all the beautiful cars I wanted to buy!

NQ: So, what happened?

EB: Kwasi helped a lot. He really taught me that money is not #1. The important things in life are family, education, and health. And I still have a lot to learn.

NQ: What exactly do you need to learn?

EB: I need to learn more about working with other people—especially with people I don't agree with.

NQ: Evan, good luck to you! Do you have a final comment for our readers?

EB: I want to be a leader like Kwasi. Thirty years from now, I want people to say "Evan Burch was—or is—a great athlete, a great leader, and a good person," not "Evan Burch was a great athlete with a lot of expensive cars when he was 18."

---

[1] **NBA:** National Basketball Association

COMPREHENSION

Write **T** (true) or **F** (false). Discuss your answers with a partner.

_____ 1. Evan Burch wants to finish college before he plays pro basketball.

_____ 2. Kwasi Rodland thinks that college is very important.

_____ 3. Kwasi Rodland thinks that money makes athletes happy.

_____ 4. Evan Burch wanted to buy lots of cars, but now he thinks cars are less important than his education.

_____ 5. Burch wants people to think that he is a good person.

■■■■■■■■■■■■■■■■■■■■■■■■■■■■■■■ **GO TO** MyEnglishLab **FOR MORE VOCABULARY PRACTICE.**

READING SKILL

1 Reread the end of Reading Two on page 178. What does Evan talk about? Check (✓) all of the correct answers.

At the end of Reading Two, Evan talks about _____.

_____ his family

_____ his hope for the future

_____ how he learned basketball

RECOGNIZING THE CONCLUSION

When we read the **conclusion**, we know that a reading will end soon. The conclusion might be just one sentence, several sentences, or a paragraph. It comes at the end of the reading. The conclusion closes the reading and often reviews the important ideas in the reading.

Writers do this in different ways. Usually, the writer returns to one or more of the main ideas. Then the writer makes a comment about it.

[main idea]
These are the reasons that I want to finish college. I have learned an important lesson: Being a good person is more important than being a basketball star.
[comment]
I can play pro when I am ready.

Some writers also give an opinion in the conclusion. Giving an opinion is another way to comment on the main idea(s).

(continued on next page)

> [opinion]
>
> *Some people may disagree, but <u>I am happy about my decision. I believe that other young athletes should wait, too.</u>*
>
> Some writers may also comment on the future in the conclusion. In Reading Two, the conclusion gives Evan's hope for the future:
>
> [hope for the future]
>
> *I want to be a leader like Kwasi. <u>Thirty years from now, I want people to say</u>*
>
> *<u>"Evan Burch was—or is—a great athlete, a great leader, and a good person," not</u>*
>
> *<u>"Evan Burch was a great athlete with a lot of expensive cars when he was 18."</u>*
>
> When you read, look for the conclusion. Recognizing and understanding the conclusion can help you understand the most important points in the reading.

2 Look at Reading One again. Reread the conclusion (paragraph 5). What do you see? Check (✓) all the correct answers. Then discuss your answers with a partner. Point to sentences in the text that helped you find your answer.

In the conclusion, the writer _____.

_____ returns to the main idea(s)

_____ gives an opinion

_____ comments on the future

■■▪■■▪■■▪■■▪■■▪■■▪■■▪■■▪■■▪■■▪■■■■ *GO TO* My English Lab *FOR MORE SKILL PRACTICE.*

CONNECT THE READINGS

STEP 1: Organize

Work with a partner. Fill in the information from each reading in the chart.

	RONNIE ELKHOULY	EVAN BURCH
1. What is he learning before he joins the professional world?	Elkhouly . . .	Burch . . .
2. Where or how is he learning these lessons?		
3. What are some difficulties that young pro players might have?		

STEP 2: Synthesize

A TV reporter is interviewing Coach Baron from the University of Eastern Nebraska and Coach Lucas from the Brock Educational Institute. Complete the interview with information from Step 1.

Coach Baron and Coach Lucas, thank you for being here. Tell us about the difficulties for a young player who goes pro.

1. Well, _____

_____

_____

2. That's right. But also, ___

_____

_____

So players need to learn more than a sport to go pro . . .

3. Yes, they need to learn

_____

_____

4. I agree. They also need to

_____

_____

And where can they learn these things?

5. They need to go _____

_____

_____

6. _____

_____

_____

GO TO MyEnglishLab *TO CHECK WHAT YOU LEARNED.*

3 FOCUS ON WRITING

VOCABULARY

REVIEW

Cross out one word, phrase, or sentence in each item that does not make sense.

1. Joe was a really good (~~cooking~~ / running / basketball) **coach**.

2. I think that Kelly **earns** (a good job / good grades in school / a lot of money).

3. The girl who takes care of our children is only 15, but she is **mature**. (She knows what to do in an emergency. / She stays calm if the kids are angry. / She talks to her boyfriend on the phone while she babysits.)

4. I want to have a big party after I **graduate** from (the supermarket / college / high school).

5. Jennifer is a very **responsible** worker. When you ask her to do something, she (forgets / does it well / makes sure the job is finished).

6. Aisha has great **talent** for (singing / walking / tennis).

7. After I graduated from high school, my family **recommended** that I (go to college / get a job / do my homework).

8. Maresa has **experience** as a pro golfer. (She can give advice to young golfers. / She doesn't like playing professional golf. / She knows how to live in the spotlight.)

9. Scott had some **difficulties** after he became a pro basketball player. (He didn't know how to deal with the media. / He hurt his arm and couldn't play any more. / He made millions of dollars.)

10. Scott also didn't know how to **deal with** the media. (He got angry with their questions. / He played basketball every day. / He got upset about their comments about him.)

11. Lydia was upset about the media's (untrue / expensive / negative) **comments**.

1 Study the sports idioms. There is one example from sports and another from everyday school life for each one.

---

hog the (ball): *keep the (ball) to yourself, control use of something, not share (something) with your group or teammates*

Mary doesn't hog the ball. She passes the ball to her teammates when necessary.

Mary doesn't hog the paint in art class. She shares with other students.

---

call the shots: *make all the decisions for a group*

Listen to the coach. He calls all the shots.

Bill is our class president. He calls all the shots on the student council.

---

get the ball rolling: *start something, like a conversation between people*

Let's get the ball rolling, team. Go out on the field and win this game!

Let's get the ball rolling, class. First, let's talk about last night's homework.

---

be / get on the ball: *be / become intelligent, focused, ready to act*

On the tennis court, Vincent is always on the ball. He thinks only about the match.

Vincent! Wake up. Get on the ball! Pay attention! We are on page 204.

---

be a team player: *work well with other people on a team or group members; cooperate with other people*

If you want to play on this team, you have to be a team player. Don't hog the ball and don't try to be a star.

If you want an "A" on your group project in this class, you have to be a team player.

Match the situations with the correct responses.

Situations

1. Bryan always listens carefully and thinks about his group's opinions. You can say: _____

2. You are working with a group of classmates. Your assignment is to discuss why Ronnie Elkhouly should or should not turn pro. You are the group leader. To begin, you say: _____

3. You want to try to score a goal, but your teammate does not pass the ball to you or anyone. You say to your teammate: _____

4. You forgot your mother's birthday, but your secretary remembered. She sent your mother some flowers. You say: _____

5. You are the captain of the soccer team, and one of your teammates isn't listening to your instruction. You tell him: _____

Responses

a. "Hey, Jimmy. Don't hog the ball!"

b. "He's a real team player."

c. "Thanks for doing that for me, Dana. You are always on the ball."

d. "OK, who wants to get the ball rolling? Debbie, how about you?"

e. "I call all the shots during the game."

Study the pictures. What are the people saying? Write their words on the line. Use the vocabulary from Expand.

Teacher: _____

Student: _____   Student: _____

Compare your answers with a partner's. Explain your choices.

GRAMMAR

1 Read each statement. Then choose the sentence that represents the meaning of the statement.

1. Some people think Elkhouly is **very mature** for his age.

   a. Elkhouly is less mature than other kids his age.

   b. Elkhouly is more mature than other kids his age.

2. Elkhouly is **too young** to play pro baseball in Japan.

   a. At his age, Elkhouly can't play pro baseball in Japan.

   b. At his age, Elkhouly can play pro baseball in Japan.

3. Kwasi Rodland is **too old** to play with the NBA.

   a. Rodland can't play with the NBA.

   b. Rodland can play with the NBA.

4. Kwasi Rodland is not **too old** to teach younger players.

   a. Rodland can't teach younger players.

   b. Rodland can teach younger players.

5. The teachers think Elkhouly is **mature enough** to play professional baseball.

   a. They think it's not OK for him to play professional baseball.

   b. They think it's OK for him to play professional baseball.

6. Evan Burch is **old enough** to join the NBA.

   a. At his age, Burch can't play in the NBA.

   b. At his age, Burch can play in the NBA.

7. Many people think that Elkhouly is not **mature enough** to turn pro.

   a. They think it's not OK for Elkhouly to turn pro at his age.

   b. They think it's OK for Elkhouly to turn pro at his age.

VERY, TOO, AND ENOUGH

Use *very* before an adjective to make the adjective stronger.

[adjective]
That car is **very expensive**. I'm not sure if I should spend so much.

Use *too* before an adjective to show a problem.

[adjective]
That car is **too expensive** for me to buy. I'll buy a less expensive one.

Use *enough* after an adjective or before a noun. Use *enough* to say something about "amount."

[adjective]
The yellow car isn't **cheap enough** for me to buy. I think I'll buy the red one.

[noun]
I have **enough money** to buy the red car,

[noun]
but I don't have **enough money** to buy the yellow one. I'll buy the red one.

These sentences have the same meaning:
The yellow car is **too expensive** for me to buy.
I don't have **enough money** to buy the yellow car.

These sentences also have the same meaning:
The red car isn't **too expensive**.
I have **enough money** to buy the red one.

2 Put the words in order to make sentences.

1. Kwasi Rodland / basketball / too / is / play / to / old / pro

Kwasi Roland is too old to play pro basketball.

2. a / is / Joe / musician / talented / very

_____

3. basketball / tall / to / is / play / enough / Kevin

_____

(continued on next page)

4. enough / drive / not / is / Jamie / old / to

_____

5. pick up / Sally / not / is / strong / enough / to / the box

_____

6. Martina / win / at / Wimbledon / enough / was / to / good

_____

3 Study the picture. Finish the sentences with the words provided. For the last two, write your own sentence about Ayala. Use **too** or **enough**.

1. Jeff / short ___Jeff is too short to ride The Sled._____

2. Jeff / young _____

3. Jeff / heavy _____

4. Charlie / tall _____

5. Charlie / heavy _____

6. Charlie / old _____

7. Ayala _____

8. Ayala _____

4 Answer the questions with **too** or **enough**.

1. What are some things that you are too old to do now?

_____

_____

2. What are some things that you are not old enough to do yet?

_____

_____

■■■■■■■■■■■ *GO TO* MyEnglishLab *FOR MORE GRAMMAR PRACTICE AND TO CHECK WHAT YOU LEARNED.*

FINAL WRITING TASK

In this unit, you read about two young athletes. Now read the short newspaper article about another young player.

You are going to **write a paragraph expressing your opinion** about this young athlete and her plan to turn pro at age 12. Use the vocabulary and grammar from the unit.*

Read about Diana Verdejo.

12-Year-Old Will Play Pro

San Rafael Observer, June 19, 2013

Diana Verdejo loves golf, and she has a lot of talent. Diana is just 12 years old, but coaches call her every year because they want her to be on their teams. Now, professional coaches are calling because they want her to get ready for their professional teams.

Diana knows that some young athletes turn pro at 14. Diana's parents say that they do not feel worried that she is too young to think about becoming a professional. They want her to do what she loves.

---

* For Alternative Writing Topics, see page 194. These topics can be used in place of the writing topic for this unit or as homework. The alternative topics relate to the theme of the unit, but may not target the same grammar or rhetorical structures taught in the unit.

PREPARE TO WRITE: Brainstorming

To help you plan your paragraph, you are going to **brainstorm** as a prewriting activity.

Work with a partner. Make a list of the pros and cons of becoming a pro athlete at a young age. Think about Ronnie Elkhouly and Evan Burch. Add your own ideas. Write the benefits in the (+) column and the drawbacks in the (−) column.

+	−

Look at the two columns. What's your opinion about Diana Verdejo?

WRITE: An Opinion

In an opinion paragraph, you express your personal ideas about a topic. You also give reasons for your opinion. To give an opinion, use the expressions in the chart.

In my opinion, + subject + verb + (the rest of the sentence)	**In my opinion,** Ronnie Elkhouly is old enough to be a professional athlete.
I think (that) + subject + *should* + main verb + (the rest of the sentence)	**I think that** Ronnie Elkhouly should become a professional athlete.
I (strongly) believe (that) + subject + verb + (the rest of the sentence) **Note:** Some people leave out **that**, especially when speaking.	**I (strongly) believe** Ronnie Elkhouly is old enough to be a professional athlete.

1 Read the paragraph. Then answer the questions.

In my opinion, Ronnie Elkhouly is old enough to be a pro athlete. He is just 16 years old, but I think he is ready. One reason I think Ronnie is old enough is that he gets support. He is not alone. Ronnie's teachers and coaches help him. They give him advice, and Ronnie listens. They gave him a job so he can learn to be responsible. Another reason is that playing pro is a good opportunity. Ronnie will earn a lot of money. In the future, he can spend his money on college. He can go to school any time, but he can play baseball only when he is young. For all these reasons, I think that Ronnie is ready.

1. What is the writer's opinion?_____

_____

2. What support does the writer give for his/her opinion?

_____

_____

2 Write the first draft of your opinion paragraph about Diana Verdejo. Give reasons for your opinion. Use the chart on page 190 to help you write your paragraph.

REVISE: Writing a Concluding Sentence

A concluding sentence is usually the last sentence of a paragraph. Often, the concluding sentence repeats or supports the main idea in the topic sentence. Sometimes the concluding sentence connects the main idea to the future.

1 Read the paragraph. Then read the four concluding sentences on the next page. Choose all the answers that fit. Explain your choice(s) to a partner.

I think that young people should play sports. One reason is that sports are good exercise. Many kids prefer watching TV and using the Internet. They don't exercise, so they become unhealthy. If kids play sports, they will exercise and feel better. Another reason is that kids become mature when they play sports. Kids learn to work hard. They learn that they cannot be late.

(continued on next page)

Concluding Sentences:

    a. For these reasons, sports are fun.

    b. For these reasons, I think kids are good athletes.

    c. For these reasons, I hope kids will play more sports.

    d. For these reasons, sports are important for young people.

2 Write the letter of the concluding sentence next to the topic sentence. Then write what type of concluding sentence it is. Write **R** (Repetition) or **F** (Future) in the third column.

TOPIC SENTENCES	CONCLUDING SENTENCES	TYPE OF CONCLUDING SENTENCES
_____ 1. Evan is a talented athlete.	a. He wants to be more than just an athlete with expensive cars.	_____
_____ 2. Evan got good advice from older players.	b. I believe that he will become a great pro player.	_____
_____ 3. Evan cares about the important things in life.	c. He has learned important lessons.	_____

3 Read the paragraphs and write concluding sentences. Share your sentences with a partner.

    1.

In my opinion, running is the best sport. I think running is the best because I can run in all types of weather. When the weather is nice, I can run in a park and see interesting things. When the weather is bad, I can run in a gym.[1] Another reason is that running is relaxing. I can run alone and listen to music. I don't feel worried about anything.

_____

_____

_____
[1] **gym:** a large room where you do exercises or training

2.

> It is important for every athlete to have a good coach. Athletes need advice about playing. A good coach can teach the athlete how to play well. Another reason is that a good coach supports the athlete. The coach can say things like, "Keep working hard!" or "You can do it!" When athletes feel tired, a good coach helps them continue.

_____

_____

4 Now look at the first draft of your paragraph. Be sure you have a concluding sentence.

GO TO MyEnglishLab *FOR MORE SKILL PRACTICE.*

EDIT: Writing the Final Draft

Go to MYENGLISHLAB and write the final draft of your paragraph. Check your grammar, spelling, capitalization, and punctuation. Check that you used some of the grammar and vocabulary from the unit. Use the checklist to help you write your final draft. Then give your paragraph to your teacher.

FINAL DRAFT CHECKLIST

❏ Did you express an opinion?

❏ Did you begin with a good topic sentence?

❏ Did you use a concluding sentence? Does it support the topic sentence?

❏ Did you use *very, too,* and *enough*?

❏ Did you use vocabulary from the unit?

UNIT PROJECT

Work in groups and find out more about a professional sports star. Make a timeline of the important events in his or her life so far.

STEP 1: With your group, decide whom to research.

STEP 2: Search the Internet. Divide up the research as follows. One person researches each of these sites:

- Websites for pro sports leagues (Major League Soccer [MLS] websites for a soccer player, Major League Baseball [MLB] websites for a baseball player, National Basketball Association [NBA] websites for a basketball player, and others)
- Sports TV sites (ESPN)
- Major newspaper sites (*New York Times, BBC Sports*)
- Major sports magazine sites (*Sports Illustrated*)

STEP 3: Bring all your information to your group and fill in a timeline for the life of your sports star. (Hint: Read the titles. Titles give important information about the articles.)

STEP 4: Share your timeline with the class.

ALTERNATIVE WRITING TOPICS

Write about one of these topics. Use the vocabulary and grammar from the unit.

1. What are some of the difficulties that professional athletes have?

2. Sometimes professional athletes do or say things that are irresponsible. Write about a professional athlete who did something that was irresponsible or immature. Why do you think he or she did it?

3. Write about a person who did something important at a young age. How did this person's life change as a result?

GO TO MyEnglishLab TO WRITE ABOUT ONE OF THE ALTERNATIVE TOPICS, WATCH A VIDEO ABOUT SPORTS FOR NON-JOCKS, AND TAKE THE UNIT 8 ACHIEVEMENT TEST.

GRAMMAR BOOK REFERENCES

NorthStar: Reading and Writing Level 1, Third Edition	Focus on Grammar Level 1, Third Edition	Azar's Basic English Grammar, Fourth Edition
Unit 1 Questions with *Be* and *Have*	**Unit 5** Present of *Be: Yes / No* Questions, Questions with *Who* and *What* **Unit 6** Present of *Be: Where* Questions **Unit 13** Simple Present *Be* and *Have*	**Chapter 2** Using *Be* and *Have*
Unit 2 Simple Past of *Be* and *Have*	**Unit 7** Past of *Be:* Statements, *Yes / No* Questions **Unit 8** Past of *Be: Wh-* Questions **Unit 23** Simple Past of Irregular Verbs	**Chapter 8** Expressing Past Time, Part 1
Unit 3 Simple Present	**Unit 10** Simple Present: Statements **Unit 11** Simple Present: *Yes / No* Questions **Unit 12** Simple Present: *Wh-* Questions	**Chapter 3** Using the Simple Present
Unit 4 *There is / There are*	**Unit 27** *There is / There are*	**Chapter 5** *There + Be:* 5-4 *There + Be Yes / No* Questions: 5-5

(continued on next page)

NorthStar: Reading and Writing Level 1, Third Edition	Focus on Grammar Level 1, Third Edition	Azar's Basic Engligh Grammar, Fourth Edition
Unit 5 Basic Modal Verbs	**Unit 21** *Can / Can't*	**Chapter 10** Expressing Future time, Part 1 **Chapter 11** Expressing Future time, Part 2 **Chapters 12** Modals, Part 1: Expressing Ability
Unit 6 Simple Past Irregular Verbs	**Unit 22** Simple Past: Regular Verbs (Statements) **Unit 23** Simple Past: Regular and Irregular Verbs; *Yes / No* Questions **Unit 24** Simple Past: *Wh-* Questions	**Chapter 8** Expressing Past Time, Part 1 **Chapter 9** Expressing Past Time, Part 2
Unit 7 Comparative Adjectives	**Unit 29** Comparative Adjectives	**Chapter 15** Making Comparisons
Unit 8 *Very, Too,* and *Enough*		**Chapter 12** Using *Very* and *Too* + Adjective: 12-7

UNIT WORD LIST

The Unit Word List is a summary of key vocabulary from the Student Book. Words followed by an asterisk (*) are on the Academic Word List (AWL).

UNIT 1

advice
chat
community*
females
goals*
laughed
males

meet
peace
personal
safe
updates
users

UNIT 2

ad
drawing
energetic*
famous
graffiti
museum

painting
posters
public
sculpture
symbol*

UNIT 3

collections
condition
experts*
favorite
guests
items*

rare
sentimental
similar*
valuable
worth

UNIT 4

artisans
crafts
customer
employee
marketplace
own
owner
personal
   attention

price
product
service
shop
shopping
unique*
vendors

(continued on next page)

UNIT 5

afraid (of)	normal*
avoid	panic
disgusting	phobia
embarrassed	relaxed*
fear	sweat
needles	

UNIT 6

adventure	media*
contest	pilot
event	risky
flight	set a record
hero	took off
landed	unforgettable

UNIT 7

adults*	neighbors
born	rules
expect	siblings
likely	spoiled
middle	stereotype
misbehave	strict

UNIT 8

coach	graduated
comments*	mature*
deal with	recommend
difficulties	responsible
earned	talent
experience	

PHOTO CREDITS

THE PHONETIC ALPHABET

Consonant Symbols			
/b/	be	/t/	to
/d/	do	/v/	van
/f/	father	/w/	will
/g/	get	/y/	yes
/h/	he	/z/	zoo, busy
/k/	keep, can	/θ/	thanks
/l/	let	/ð/	then
/m/	may	/ʃ/	she
/n/	no	/ʒ/	vision, Asia
/p/	pen	/tʃ/	child
/r/	rain	/dʒ/	join
/s/	so, circle	/ŋ/	long

Vowel Symbols			
/ɑ/	far, hot	/iy/	we, mean, feet
/ɛ/	met, said	/ey/	day, late, rain
/ɔ/	tall, bought	/ow/	go, low, coat
/ə/	son, under	/uw/	too, blue
/æ/	cat	/ay/	time, buy
/ɪ/	ship	/aw/	house, now
/ʊ/	good, could, put	/oy/	boy, coin